D0866367

The Printed Book

CAMBRIDGE
UNIVERSITY PRESS
LONDON: BENTLEY HOUSE
NEW YORK TORONTO BOMBAY
CALCUTTA MADRAS: MACMILLAN
TOKYO: MARUZEN COMPANY LTD

THE PRINTED BOOK

by

HARRY G. ALDIS

❦

The Second Edition
Revised & brought up to date
by

JOHN CARTER
and
E. A. CRUTCHLEY

CAMBRIDGE

AT THE UNIVERSITY PRESS

1941

First published in the Cambridge Manuals of Science and Literature	1916
Reprinted	1917, 1921, 1929
New Edition	1941

PRINTED IN GREAT BRITAIN BY WALTER LEWIS
AT THE UNIVERSITY PRESS, CAMBRIDGE

PREFACE

TO THE NEW EDITION

It has been the editors' endeavour, in the revision of this manual, to preserve as much as possible of the original framework and approach. The author's survey of the earlier history of the printed book required very few changes to bring it up to date, though the researches of the intervening twenty-five years necessitated certain minor modifications, e.g. in the attribution of the forty-two line Bible and the estimate of the typographical importance of Aldus Manutius.

Aldis's account of 'The Modern Book', however, was too strongly tinged with the prejudices and predilections of his own day to be satisfactory to readers who have come to realize that the period between Bensley and William Morris is not wholly without interest; and both this and the following chapter have been substantially rewritten. The main changes in the chapter on 'Illustrations' were dictated by similar considerations, while recent work on the dark history of edition binding made it necessary to recast and amplify the latter part of Chapter IX.

The subject of the final chapter allowed free play to Aldis's vigorous and characteristic expression of his own tastes. To intrude on these was something of an impertinence, and in only one particular was the editors' disagreement so violent as to compel them to do so. They can only hope that the strength of their feelings on this particular point is expressed with a sufficiently Aldisian warmth to engage the sympathy, if not the respect, of the author.

Six new illustrations have been inserted and three omitted from those appearing in the earlier edition. Thanks are due to the Cambridge University Library, the Bodleian, the Fitzwilliam Museum, and Mr Michael Sadleir for allowing books in their possession to be photographed; and to Mr C. H. St John Hornby, Linotype and Machinery Ltd., and the Monotype Corporation Ltd., for their help with the appendix on the development of type faces.

JOHN CARTER
E. A. CRUTCHLEY

October 1940

CONTENTS

ILLUSTRATIONS

All the illustrations, except those facing page 16, *are reduced in reproduction*

Caxton's device

CHAPTER I

THE ADVENT OF PRINTING

The year of the fall of Constantinople, 1453, is generally considered the dividing line between the medieval and the modern periods of history. But about that same time another event was taking place which, though not heralded by clash of arms or ruin of empires, affords an equally significant landmark—the invention of printing with movable types. It would be difficult to point to any discovery which has had so far-reaching an influence upon the history of the world: and it is a curious reflection that printing began so quietly, so unobtrusively, that not only can no precise year be assigned to it, but, like more than one important discovery of even recent times, the individual to be honoured as its inventor, and actually the country of its origin, have been matters of dispute.

The art of printing with movable metal types was preceded by the production of single pictures printed from wood-blocks. One of the earliest of these which bears a date is the St Christopher of 1423, now in the John Rylands Library at Manchester. It seems a natural development that lines of descriptive text should be added to such woodcuts; and the 'block-books', which consist of pictures and text cut on the same wood-block, have usually been regarded as occupying a position midway between the single picture and the book printed from movable type, thus forming a link in the evolution of the invention.

These block-books, or xylographica, of which upwards of a hundred issues and editions, comprising some thirty separate works, have been recorded, were produced chiefly in the Netherlands and Germany. They fall into two classes. The earlier were printed in thin pale brownish ink on one side of the leaf only. They were produced by placing a sheet of paper upon the inked block and transferring the image to the paper by friction on the back of the sheet with a burnisher or some similar instrument, without mechanical pressure. The other and later class were usually printed in a press with ordinary black printing ink and on both sides of the paper.

Since the contents of each individual page had to be engraved upon a block of wood, the making of a block-book was a laborious process, and one suitable only for works of moderate length for which there was a large and continuous demand. These books were, accordingly, of a popular nature, mainly concerned with religious instruction or pious edification, and lending themselves readily to pictorial or allegorical illustration. Typical examples are the *Biblia Pauperum*, a series of pictures from the life of Christ, accompanied by parallel subjects from the Old Testament; the *Apocalypse*, an attractive subject for illustrations; and *Ars Moriendi*, a series of pictures representing the trials which beset the dying and the spiritual helps by which they may be overcome.

While this method of reproduction was fairly convenient for the class of work for which it was used, it was quite inadequate to the cheap and speedy multiplication of that type of book which the revival of literature and learning was demanding.

The immense superiority of typography over xylography lay in the fact that while the xylographic blocks could be used only for the particular work for which they had been cut, the movable type, being composed of separate letters, could be used over and over again for any book, with corresponding economy both in time and in material. It was an epoch-making difference.

The precise details of when, where, and by whom printing with movable type was first invented are veiled in a considerable obscurity. The claims of Germany, Holland, and even France, to priority have been advanced with much zeal, edged occasionally with more than a touch of acrimony: and indeed the faint light shed by contemporary record affords plenty of room for ingenious argument and special pleading. Nevertheless, the references to the subject found in books before the end of the fifteenth century agree generally in attributing the invention to Johann Gensfleisch zum Gutenberg of Mainz, even though some of them are obviously inaccurate in detail. The earliest known reference to Gutenberg being at work on the process of printing occurs in the record of a Strasbourg lawsuit of 1439, in which a goldsmith testified to having sold him what were clearly printing materials in 1436.

What is termed the 'Haarlem legend', which attributes the discovery to Laurens Janszoon Coster of Haarlem about the year 1440, does not emerge until the second half of the sixteenth century; but it receives a certain amount of support from the story of the invention as related, on the authority of Ulrich Zell, the printer, in the *Cologne Chronicle* printed in 1499. This account says that the art was first invented at Mainz about 1440; that for the next ten years it was being investigated; and that in 1450 men began to print. But it goes on to say that 'Although this art was invented at Mainz as far as regards the manner in which it is now commonly used, yet the first prefiguration (Vurbyldung) was invented in Holland from the Donatuses which were printed there before that time'.*

The *Donatus* here spoken of is the *De octo partibus orationis* of Aelius Donatus, the fourth-century grammarian; a book as familiar to the schoolboy of the middle ages as *Euclid* was to the schoolboy of yesterday. Of these early *Donatuses*, which are regarded as being among the very first productions of the press, fragments of some twenty editions printed in Holland and about sixteen printed in Germany have survived. Unfortunately it did not occur to the printer of any of them that by adding his name and the date he might achieve immortality.

Whether Holland or Germany be the rightful claimant to priority in some kind of printing, there is little doubt that the invention of the effective process may be referred to the decade 1440–50; and that it was at Strasbourg and Mainz that it was first developed to a practical issue.

Three men were involved—Johann Gutenberg, Johann Fust and Peter Schoeffer; and discussion has long raged over the part which each played in the invention and establishment of the new process. On the basis of the evidence at present available, however, we may say with confidence that Gutenberg was the in-

* A. W. Pollard, *Fine Books* (1912), pp. 34ff., where the passage is printed in full.

ventor of printing with movable types cast from matrices (the essential factor in the whole business). Fust, a lawyer and financier of Mainz, put up capital for Gutenberg during the experimental period, but foreclosed on the partnership before it produced substantial (or certainly datable) fruit, and combined instead with his son-in-law, Schoeffer. Gutenberg's name is not found in the colophon of any known piece of printing. But he is confidently believed to have been solely responsible for one substantial early achievement, the thirty-six line Bible, and for the majority of those minor products of the press which certainly precede the long accepted 'first printed book'—popularly known as the Mazarine or Gutenberg Bible, but more safely and correctly as the forty-two line Bible.

The probably considerable output of the experimental period has survived only in a few fragments, tentatively arranged as follows: (1) *The Fragment of the World Judgment*; part of a single leaf of a Sibylline poem in German, of which the complete book would have run to thirty-seven leaves. This has been attributed to a date between 1444 and 1447 but only on the debatable evidence of type-state. (2) *An Astronomical Calendar*, calculated for 1448. This is much the most important of these pieces, since it must quite clearly have been printed late in 1447 or early in 1448, and its type is that of the thirty-six line Bible. (3) A number of issues of *Donatus*, the earliest assigned to printing dates no more definite than 'before 1458'. (4) The twelve-page pamphlet, *A warning to Christendom against the Turks*, which seems to have been printed in December 1454: this also is attributed to Gutenberg. (5) A *Calendar* for the year 1457, printed in the thirty-six line Bible type.

By the end of 1454, however, Fust had broken with Gutenberg, and two parallel *Indulgences* provide the first evidence of the existence of a rival press. The thirty-one line *Indulgence* was printed before 14 November 1454, on which date a copy was used at Erfurt. Key words are printed in Gutenberg's thirty-six line Bible type. The thirty-line *Indulgence* was printed before 27 February 1455, on which date a copy was used at Cologne. Key words are printed in the type of the forty-two line Bible. The attribution of this second *Indulgence* to the new firm of Fust and Schoeffer is hardly disputable; and it is noteworthy that its significant type is later found in the possession of Peter Schoeffer, who carried on alone after Fust's death in 1466.

From this shadowy and speculative period we suddenly emerge upon a fully fledged masterpiece of the printer's art. When on 24 August 1456 Heinrich Cremer, vicar of St Stephen's Church at Mainz, recorded in a magnificent copy of the Bible* the fact that the rubrication and binding of the book was then finished, he expressed his pride and satisfaction at the completion of the two fine volumes. He little realized the importance this date would assume in connection with the revolutionary technique by which the text of his book had been produced. The book was in fact a copy of the forty-two line Bible, the first large book to issue from the press. It still bears neither printer's name nor date of printing; but Cremer's inscription in the Paris copy shows that it must have been published before August 1456.

* Now in the Bibliothèque Nationale at Paris.

This famous and splendid book was long attributed to Gutenberg, chiefly on the ground that it was the first book and he the first printer. Even since the discovery, at Wiesbaden in 1901, of the 1448 *Calendar*, he has been widely credited with at least its planning and inception. Yet that document proves that he was in possession of a Bible-size type from 1448 to 1457 (when his *Calendar* was printed), which makes it unreasonable to suppose that he would have involved himself, even if he had the funds, in the very heavy expense of a second large-size type. Common sense, meanwhile, denies probability to the picture of Gutenberg—deprived of his financial backing and defaulter on a court judgment in favour of his ex-backer—undertaking two Bibles at the same time, one of them (the forty-two line) printed on six presses.

Fust and Schoeffer, on the other hand, had plenty of money (Fust's) and plenty of typographical ability (Schoeffer's). They had begun printing at least as early as January 1455. The Bible was an obvious choice for the first full-size book, even if Gutenberg's start on his thirty-six line Bible had not suggested it.* The dates allow well over a year for the completion of the project; and the forty-two line Bible type was already in their possession. On the evidence at present available, therefore, it seems a reasonable inference that the Mazarine, Gutenberg, or forty-two line Bible was printed by Fust and Schoeffer.

* The larger part of this seems to have been set up from a copy of the forty-two line Bible: but not the first few sheets, which may therefore be presumed to have been printed before the appearance of the other.

Supremacy in the new art, in fact, had already passed from the inventor to his better organized rivals; even though Gutenberg was probably the printer of an impressive folio dated 1460, the Mainz *Catholicon*. Schoeffer's genius was even more effectively demonstrated in 1457 by the appearance of the celebrated *Psalter*, the first book to contain printer's name and date. This was an astonishing *tour de force* for an infant craft, and indeed a piece of bookmaking which would have been striking in any period: being executed in red and black throughout, with large floriated initials printed in two colours, impeccably registered.

Printing had come of age, and with a flourish.

CHAPTER II

THE SPREAD OF THE ART

For a few years Mainz held a monopoly of printing, but by 1458 it had been carried to Strasbourg and by 1461 to Bamberg; and soon, aided probably by the disturbed state of Mainz in 1462, it spread to other places. At Cologne, Ulrich Zell, who set up a press there in 1465, was followed by upwards of thirty other craftsmen before the end of the century. Three years later Gunther Zainer produced the first dated Augsburg book, and the incunabula printed at this important home of woodcutting include a considerable number of illustrated works. Nuremberg saw its first press (Sensenschmidt) in 1470. The most prolific printer in that busy centre of the book trade was Anton Koberger, printer of that best-selling picture-book the *Nuremberg Chronicle* of 1493. Other towns followed in rapid succession, and by the end of the century printing had been practised in fifty-one towns in Germany.

In the meantime the invention had found its way into other countries. Italy received it* at the hands of two Germans, Conrad Sweynheym and Arnold Pannartz, who in 1465 set up a press in the Benedictine monastery at Subiaco. Here the roman letter was born, beating by a short head the Adolf Rusch fount long regarded as the first. After printing four books, however, the first of

* An unknown travelling craftsman, about 1464, printed the first book on Italian soil; set in a rounded form of gothic.

which was the inevitable *Donatus*,* these printers moved on to Rome in 1467. Apparently success did not attend their enterprise, for in March 1472 they sought the aid of Pope Sixtus IV. Their plea, which discloses some interesting details about the operation of their press, gives a list of the twenty-eight different works they had up to that time printed, with the number of copies of each, usually 275. Including separate editions of these twenty-eight books, they had printed in all a total of 11,475 volumes.

Rome was followed by Venice in 1469, and more printers worked in Venice during the fifteenth century than in any other town. These, about 150 in number, included Nicolas Jenson, a Frenchman whose much admired roman type was too often spoiled by indifferent presswork; Erhard Ratdolt, from Augsburg, whose books, mainly mathematical and astronomical, are adorned with some particularly fine ornamental borders; Bonetus Locatellus, whose productions are more numerous than interesting; and Aldus Manutius, of world-wide fame. At Milan, which in company with Florence, Naples and four other Italian towns first adopted the art in 1471, was published the earliest dated book printed entirely in Greek, the *Grammar* of Lascaris (1476); and the *editio princeps* of Homer issued from a Florence press (probably that of Bartholomaeus de Libris) in 1488. Printing now spread very rapidly through Italy, the pioneers in many cases being Germans; and by the year 1500 presses had been at work in more than seventy different towns south of the Alps.

France also learned its printing from German work-

* No copy is known to survive.

men. It was at the instance of two of the professors that Martin Crantz, Ulrich Gering and Michael Friburger set up a press at the Sorbonne in 1470, and Paris soon became a busy centre of the book trade. The only other French towns in which printing was carried on to any considerable extent during the century were Lyons and Rouen, the latter of which became notable for the production of books of hours and other liturgical works.

Of other European countries Switzerland was early in the field, Ruppel beginning to work at Basel in 1468. Bohemia had its first press at Pilsen in 1468, its second at Prague ten years later. Hungary followed, with Hesse of Budapesth, in 1473 or 1474; Poland in 1474; and the same year saw the first Spanish press set up at Valencia by Palmart, a Fleming.

In Holland it is known that printing by the Gutenberg process began at Utrecht about 1470, though the earliest book bearing a date is the *Historia scholastica* of Petrus Comestor, printed there in 1473. But the Dutch editions of *Donatus*, mentioned in the preceding chapter, to which no certain date can be attached, together with a few other books belonging to the same group, are quite possibly earlier than this. Haarlem, claimed as the scene of the shadowy Coster's operations, produced no recorded printer until ten years after the Utrecht press had been started, and in the meantime printing had been introduced into some fifteen other towns in the Low Countries. The most important centres of early printing in Holland and Belgium were Deventer and Louvain; but Bruges possesses a special interest since it was there that William Caxton, England's first printer, worked in partnership with Colard Mansion for two or three years before he returned to England to introduce printing to his native country.

Caxton was, as he himself states, born and brought up in the Weald of Kent. After serving an apprenticeship to a mercer in London he migrated to the south Netherlands, where by 1463 he was established in the important office of Governor of the English Nation in the Low Countries. In 1471 he was living in Cologne, and probably there gained a technical knowledge of printing. He returned to Bruges and with Colard Mansion, a professional calligrapher, acquired printing materials; and together they printed at least three books in 1474–6, one of which, Caxton's own translation of the *Recuyell of the Historyes of Troye* (1474), was the first book printed in the English language. Some time in 1476 Caxton returned to England, and, establishing himself at Westminster at Michaelmas, set up the first English press at the sign of the 'Red Pale', under the shadow of the Abbey. That he lost no time in getting to work is proved by the date on the earliest known product of the English printing press, an *Indulgence*, with the issue date filled in on 13 December 1476. It is generally agreed that several of his small undated quartos belong to the year 1477, but the earliest dated Caxton is the *Dictes or Sayengis of the Philosophres*, translated from the French by Earl Rivers, and finished on 18 November 1477. By the end of the following year he had printed upwards of twenty books, and at least five times that number before his death, which occurred some time in 1491.

Caxton, though his books have not much claim to beauty, was no mere mechanical producer. He took upon himself the labours of translator and editor as well; and it is likely that it was a love of books and a leaning towards literature that induced him to take up printing. The Bruges *Troy* book was his own translation; to the *Dictes*, which he edited, he added a chapter concerning women; and he early turned his attention to producing an edition of the *Canterbury Tales*, the first English printing of a native classic. He printed for the English market, with probably a strong bias towards what most pleased his personal taste, and the majority of his books have a distinctly literary character. Commercial acumen, no doubt, supported him in this course, since the limited demand for the more serious works required by the scholar and the student would scarcely have justified printing them in England, especially as good editions could be readily imported from the continent. Consequently classics, standard theological treatises and the ponderous excogitations of the schoolmen are practically absent from the list of his publications. On the other hand, his many volumes of poetry and romance must have stimulated the demand for such literature; while at the same time by his own translations from the French he enlarged the bounds of English recreative reading.

Caxton did not long remain the sole printer in England. Theodoric Rood was at work in Oxford with Cologne types from 1478 to 1485; and an unknown, called 'the schoolmaster printer', had produced eight books at St Albans by 1485. The first London press was that of John Lettou, who soon after his commencement in 1480 was joined by William de Machlinia. They printed chiefly law books.

At Westminster Caxton was succeeded by his chief assistant, Wynkyn de Worde, who carried on the traditions of the press in so far as a large proportion of his books consisted of romances and verse. But, unlike his master, de Worde was a mere printer and showed no trace of literary talent. His finest book, an English version of the *De proprietatibus rerum* of Bartholomaeus Anglicus (about 1496), was the first book to be printed on paper made in England. De Worde died about the beginning of the year 1535. During his long career he is known to have printed between seven and eight hundred books, but many of these were short popular works and a large number were merely new editions.

Richard Pynson, Wynkyn de Worde's chief contemporary, printed in London from about 1490 to 1530. As befitted the office of King's Printer he possessed the best-appointed printing house of his time in England. His output consisted to a large extent of law books and official work; but he also printed many books of literary interest, such as the *Canterbury Tales*, Barclay's English version of Brant's *Ship of Fools*, and Lord Berners's translation of Froissart's *Chronicles*, besides several liturgical books of very respectable workmanship. The only other English printer in the fifteenth century was Julian Notary, who began in London about 1496 and was active for nearly a quarter of a century.

Caxton's successors adopted the French *lettre de forme* as their normal type, and this became the traditional English 'black letter'. 'Roman' was first imported from Paris by Pynson in 1509.

CHAPTER III

THE FIFTEENTH-CENTURY BOOK

It requires some effort to realize that before the invention of printing all books were in manuscript and that the laborious process of writing out each separate copy was the normal means of reproducing a work. This business of making manuscript copies of books was carried on not only in the monastic *scriptoria* and other homes of scholarship, but was also followed as a regular profession; and in a great centre of learning, such as Paris, a vast number of calligraphers, rubricators, illuminators, binders, and others of kindred calling gained their daily living by this industry.

To make twenty manuscript copies of a book was practically twenty times the work of making one copy; but in the printing of a book, when once the type is set up, any number of copies can be produced with comparatively little additional labour. It was this tedious business of writing out every separate additional copy that impressed Caxton with the advantages of printing. For having, as he relates in his *Recuyell of the Historyes of Troye*, promised copies of the book 'to dyverce gentilmen and to my frendes', 'in the wrytyng of the same my penne is worn, myn hande wery and not stedfast, myn eyen dimmed with overmoche lokyng on the whit paper...therefore I have practysed and lerned at my grete charge and dispense to ordeyne this said book in prynte after the manner and forme as ye may here see'.

The primary effect of the invention of printing was to render multiplication of copies of a book cheaper and more expeditious. It was, of course, a manuscript that the early printer had in his mind's eye: the production of a number of copies which as nearly as possible resembled a manuscript in appearance; and indeed, an early printed book often looks so like a manuscript of the same work written in the formal book-hand, that, if the two are placed side by side, an unpractised eye finds some difficulty in distinguishing between them.

In designing his types, as the letters used in printing are called, the pioneer printer naturally followed the formal book-hand used in the district in which he was working, or the special hand customarily employed in the particular class of book which he proposed to print. Latin Bibles and liturgical works were generally printed in the black letter, which, under the unifying influence of the Church, had become habitual in writing books for use in her services. In Germany varying forms of gothic text were adopted; while the round minuscule writing affected by Italian scribes formed the model for the roman type so widely favoured in Italy. Caxton's first types, of course, reflected their origin—the ordinary Flemish book-hand which he was accustomed to see in manuscripts during his residence in the Low Countries.

In the early days of typography it was usual for the printer to print only the bare text; just that part of the book which, in a manuscript, would be written by the scribe or calligrapher. Blank spaces were left for headlines, initial letters, and other ornamental details, which, as in the case of manuscripts, were afterwards added by the rubricator and the illuminator. The fact that these decorative features were executed by the same craftsmen contributes to the similarity of appearance presented by the manuscript and the printed book.

The finishing adornment of a book might be more or less elaborate, from simple red or blue capitals to finely illuminated borders and historiated initials in gold and colours. Like the binding of the volume, it was no doubt generally adjusted to suit the taste and purse of the purchaser; but books are frequently found which have never been through the rubricator's hands, the pages being still in the same state in which they left the press. In these cases it will sometimes be noticed that the initial letter to be inserted is indicated by a small letter, called a director or guide letter, printed in the blank space as a guide to the illuminator. A few printers attempted to dispense with the aid of the rubrisher by printing the capitals and head-lines in red. This was a troublesome and not always successful process, in spite of the technical mastery shown in the Fust and Schoeffer *Psalter* of 1457.

The practice of leaving blank spaces for the large capitals to be filled in by hand continued in vogue in some degree throughout the fifteenth century and indeed even into the sixteenth, more particularly in Italy. But the progressive printer was not slow to perceive the advantage of sending out a book complete from the press, and the use of woodcut ornamental initial letters printed in black along with the text soon became general. Borders and other decorative pieces in imitation of the ornament of manuscripts were also brought into use, in many cases with excellent effect. Some of these borders and initials, such as the outline letters found in books printed by Anton Sorg at Augsburg, were obviously intended to be painted over by the illuminator, the skeleton design rendering his part of the work more expeditious.

In yet another respect do early printed books often resemble manuscripts. The scribe on completing his copy would usually add 'Finis' or perhaps 'Explicit', followed by the name of the work and sometimes that of the author; but he seldom went so far as to add his own name or the date. So, too, a large number of incunabula—as books printed in the fifteenth century are frequently called*—contain no intimation of when, where, or by whom they were printed. The *Psalter* of 1457 again provides the earliest exception. At the end is a paragraph stating that the book had been fashioned by the ingenious invention of printing without any writing by pen, by the diligence of Johann Fust, a citizen of Mainz, and Peter Schoeffer of Gernsheim, and brought to a completion on the Vigil of the Feast of the Assumption in the year 1457.

The early books, too, had no title-page, and the information which we now look for on that page—author, title, publisher and date—when given at all, is usually to be found, as in the *Psalter*, in the 'colophon', as this paragraph at the end of a book is called. The colophon is often accompanied by a pictorial or allegorical device which the printer had adopted as a trade-mark. Title-pages did not come into fashion until about 1480, and at first consisted of one or two lines containing merely the title of the book and perhaps the name of the author, placed in the upper part of the leaf: something like a

* 'Incunabula' means, literally, things belonging to the cradle.

fuller form of the modern half-title. The tempting blank space below this is sometimes filled in with the printer's device, or, in the case of a book printed for a bookseller, by the device of the latter. Failing a device, the page may display a woodcut illustration more or less relevant to the subject-matter of the book. The title-pages of Wynkyn de Worde's numerous small quarto tracts usually take this form, and his selection of a woodcut was beautifully casual. A grotesque attempt at the appropriate is seen in the title-page of his edition of Lydgate's *The Assembly of Gods,* which is adorned with a woodcut from an edition of Chaucer's *Canterbury Tales* depicting the company of pilgrims all seated at a huge round table.

The printer's device just referred to was at first mainly regarded as a trade-mark. The earliest, that in Fust and Schoeffer's Bible of 1462, consists of two shields suspended from a branch. The devices of the Italian printers are distinguished by beauty of ornamental design: those which consist of some variety of the combination of circle and cross in white on a black or red ground being singularly effective. In France, where they are perhaps most numerous, these devices developed in pictorial and decorative character, especially in the early part of the sixteenth century. One of the best known is the anchor and dolphin of Aldus of Venice, which made its first appearance in 1502. Among other notable examples are the fleur-de-lis of the Giuntas, Sessa's cat, Froben's twined snakes, the tree of knowledge of the Estiennes, de Colines's Time with his scythe, the compass of Plantin of Antwerp, and, somewhat later, the sphere of the Elzevirs. A favourite form in France, as well as in this country, was the canting device, containing a punning allusion to the name of the printer: the galley of the Paris printer Galliot du Pré; the griffin of Gryphius of Lyons; the mill and miller of Scotland's first printer, Andrew Myllar; and the tun embodied in the devices of Grafton, Norton, and other English printers whose names ended in 'ton'. Badius Ascensius, the sixteenth-century scholar-printer of Paris, adopted as his mark a scene in a printing office with a press at work. John of Westphalia, a busy printer at Louvain from 1474 to 1496, occasionally used a small woodcut portrait of himself; and the English Elizabethan printer John Day also displayed his portrait, but in larger and handsomer fashion. Besides this, Day had another device, depicting a sleeper being awakened, with the motto 'Arise, for it is Day'. It was not till near the end of his career that Caxton made use of his well-known bold device, reproduced at the beginning of this book.

For a time the sizes of printed books followed the lead set by manuscripts. Bibles, books of canon law and the commentaries of the schoolmen were usually ponderous volumes in large folio. What may be called the two standard sizes were the ordinary folio, standing about 12 inches high, used for books that could pretend to any importance; and the quarto, measuring about 7½ by 6 inches, a favourite size for works of small extent or popular character. An especially large number of these quartos were printed by Ulrich Zell, the first printer in Cologne, and by Richard Paffroed and Jacobus de Breda, the two fifteenth-century printers at Deventer. Smaller sizes were comparatively uncommon, and were generally reserved for books of devotion and similar religious works.

Various estimates have been made of the number of different books and editions printed in the fifteenth century, and some have even attempted to compute the total number of volumes printed: the latter a rather fruitless speculation. It is of more interest to know that of the whole output at present recorded (something over 38,000 editions) approximately rather more than one-third was produced in Italy, about one-third in Germany, while somewhat less than a third represents the combined effort of all the other countries.

CHAPTER IV

THE SCHOLAR-PRINTERS OF THE SIXTEENTH CENTURY

By the end of the fifteenth century printing had freed itself from the leading strings of the manuscript and had begun to develop its own characteristics. The book by now usually proclaims its identity: displaying on a title-page its subject, the name of its author and the address of the bookseller by whom it is published. Generally the date is also given, though this is sometimes relegated to the colophon which is still retained for recording the name of the printer, who by this time was often distinct from the publisher. Pagination, head-lines, lists of contents or chapters and other aids to ready use are commonly found, and in its main features the book differs in no material respect from the book of to-day.

The most striking and far-reaching innovation of the early years of the sixteenth century, and one of the most pregnant in the whole development of the printed book, was the introduction of a small compact type, the use of which enabled books to be reduced to a handy size. At this time, indeed, interest in the technical evolution of the book gives place to consideration of the printing press as an aid to the expansion of learning and literature, and later an instrument for the popular diffusion of knowledge. The dominant feature of the sixteenth-century press is the succession of scholar-printers who in various centres—Aldus in Venice, Froben in Basel, Badius and the Estiennes in Paris, Plantin in Antwerp—by their learning, character and influence directed its power into channels which both encouraged and satisfied the prodigious Renaissance appetite for learning.

From the outset of his career as a printer (1494–1515) Aldus Manutius devoted his energies to the cause of scholarship: to such purpose that he probably did more than any other one man to facilitate the spread of the new learning into every corner of Europe. Most of the masterpieces of ancient Greek literature made their first appearance over his imprint—imagine publishing, within a single decade, the first editions of Aristotle, Aristophanes, Aeschylus, Sophocles, Euripides, Demosthenes, Herodotus and Pindar!—but the work by which he is most widely known is the long series of small octavo volumes of Greek and Latin classics bearing the familiar device of the Aldine anchor. It was doubtless a scholar's sympathetic understanding of the need for a form of book which, by its cheapness and handy size, might become the personal belonging and intimate companion of the student, that led the printer to this radical innovation. He brought the printed book from the library to the pocket: and the change of function compelled a change of form. For the inevitable compression called for a type very different from the large roman or gothic letter used for the folios of the library and the cloister; and between 1499 and 1500 Aldus had cut for him a small new type the form of which was based on the cursive form of *antiqua* hand then current in Italy.

In his Greek type he had already deserted as his model the more or less formal contemporary book-hand, in favour of the ordinary script used for correspondence and business. These innovations were typographically unfortunate. The Aldine Greek, which reproduces all the flourishes and contractions natural to the running pen, systematically violates the first principle of type-design —legibility—and its wide influence set a disastrous fashion. Similarly his original version of the letter which we call 'italic', though extremely compact and therefore suited to its purpose in the Aldine books, is somewhat cramped in appearance and awkwardly sloped. Here again, however, the new design was received with much favour, was extensively copied, and retained great popularity, especially for small books, throughout the sixteenth century. Its long start and the Aldine prestige prevented any general adoption of the more shapely, less sloping and almost equally compact italics which were later derived by Arrighi and others from the more stylised cursive hand.

It is curious that, whereas his own and the immediately succeeding ages bestowed the compliment of frequent imitation on Aldus's greek, italic and roman impartially, nineteenth-century connoisseurship extolled the two first, which are mediocre, while completely ignoring the last. To-day, however, the Aldine roman is recognized as perhaps the finest produced in the fifteenth century; certainly the direct parent of the magnificent and widely influential designs of that later master of type-cutting, Claude Garamond.

Spain did not produce any scholar-printers in the sixteenth century. But the Spanish town of Alcalà gave to the world one scholarly and magnificent book which no historian can ignore — the great Complutensian

Polyglot Bible. Promoted and financed by Cardinal Ximenes, edited by the learned if pedantic Stunica, this vast undertaking was completed, over a period of about ten years, in six folio volumes. In the New Testament volume, for which a lordly new type had been cut, the original Greek text was printed for the first time: but although completed in 1514 (and the Old Testament in 1517) it was held up until 1522, and John Froben of Basel, hurrying out Erasmus's careless and ill-founded edition in 1516, secured the honour and profit of prior publication.

Basel had already been a centre of printing for some twenty years when Froben, who was to become its greatest printer, published in 1491 as his first book an octavo Bible in small gothic type. His press is remarkable for the number and importance of its productions, as well as for excellence of workmanship. In his desire for accuracy Froben surrounded himself with a number of scholars to whom he deputed the work of editing and correcting. Chief among these was Erasmus, who, after visiting him on several occasions, in 1521 took up permanent residence with the printer and gave fresh impetus to his press. It was in the same year as the publication of the Erasmus Greek Testament that Froben issued the works of St Jerome in nine folio volumes; and when in 1527 he met his death by a fall from an upper window, his largest undertaking, the works of St Augustine in ten folio volumes, was passing through the press.

In Froben's later years his most considerable contemporary in Basel was Adam Petri, who printed many works in the vernacular and favoured the writings of

Luther and the reformers. But more prominent centres of printing in the cause of the reformers were Geneva, the Calvinist stronghold; Zurich, where Christopher Froschauer, printer of many English books, including the first edition of the Bible in English (1535), was busy with Zwinglian literature; and Wittenberg, where Lutheran tracts came almost daily from the press of Hans Lufft. Later in the century the reputation of Basel as a centre of printing and publishing was upheld by another learned printer, John Oporinus (d. 1568), who had for four years acted as assistant to Paracelsus. Oporinus is said to have printed upwards of seven hundred books, and at one time to have employed more than fifty workmen. It was in his office that John Foxe, of the *Book of Martyrs*, was engaged as reader of the press during his sojourn at Basel.

The achievements of Aldus were not only recognized by the scholarly world: they also stirred the admiration and emulation of contemporary craftsmen. This emulation sometimes took the fairly legitimate form of an approximation of format and type, as for instance with the Giuntas of Florence. Frequently, too, an Aldine text served as 'copy' for publishers of easy conscience to reprint—piracy is perhaps too severe a term for a period when the idea of legal property in literature had scarcely been formulated. In some cases this tacit compliment to a superior editorial standard was given voice in the phrase 'ex editione Aldina', as who should say, an imitation, but from the best procurable original. Others, however, and notably the Lyonnese, were entirely unscrupulous: producing full-blooded imitations complete with false Aldine imprint—even, in the

Catullus of *c.* 1503, reproducing the misprint on the title-page—and marketing them as originals.

On the death of Aldus Greek and Latin verses were composed in his honour by his distinguished contemporary Henri Estienne, who during the first two decades of the sixteenth century shared with Jodocus Badius Ascensius the honours of Paris printing. Many of the books which Badius published contain a preface written by himself. In one of these he declares it to be his aim to emulate the laudable exactness of Aldus; and his reputation for correctness made his imprint popular among scholars. During his busy career of thirty-three years (1503–35) he printed more than seven hundred books, including almost all the Latin classics and a number of important contemporary works. Many of these bear on the title-page his well-known device of a printing press at work, with the legend *Prelum Ascensianum*.

Henri Estienne, or, in the Latin form of the name, Henricus Stephanus, was the first of an illustrious family of printers who worked in Paris for more than a century and a half. He also was famed for the accuracy of his texts. After his death in 1520, Simon de Colines, who married his widow, carried on the business until 1526, when it was handed over to Robert, Henri Estienne's second son: de Colines embarking on an independent career with a number of singularly beautiful books to his credit. This Robert was not only the most distinguished member of the family both for scholarship and for the importance of his publications: he is perhaps the most eminent in the whole list of French printers. His family circle included several scholars who were engaged in the editorial work of the press; and Latin is said to have become the ordinary language of the household from cellar to garret.

At this period the cause of learning and letters in France owed much to the patronage of King Francis I. It owed nothing at all to the theologians of Sorbonne, whose antipathy to the new learning was so bigoted that in 1533 they endeavoured to persuade the King to forbid printing in France altogether. Robert Estienne, whose editions of the Bible and other books which favoured the spread of knowledge and enlightenment brought him into conflict with the champions of ignorance, received encouragement and protection at the hands of the sovereign, and in 1539 he was nominated printer to the King in Hebrew and Latin. Francis I also commanded a new set of Greek types; and under the skilful cutting of Claude Garamond the *Grecs du Roi* proved that the Aldine-style cursive could flower into a design of extraordinary grace, virtuosity and precision. Estienne's folio *New Testament* of 1550, which shows all three sizes, is one of the most beautiful books of the century. Yet it was a fatal beauty, for the triumph of the Royal types prolonged for another two hundred years the enslavement of Greek printing to the cursive tradition. After the accession of Henry II in 1547 the royal protection was less effective, and the persistent opposition of the theologians at length drove Estienne to quit Paris for the more liberal atmosphere of Geneva. He died in 1559, leaving a flourishing business to his eldest son Henri, who was in his turn one of the great scholars of his time.

If Lyons in the early part of the sixteenth century had

earned notoriety by its piracies of Aldine and other desirable editions of the classics, the work of Sebastian Gryphius (*c.* 1524–56) gave it a more worthy reputation in the annals of printing. Gryphius strongly favoured italic types (so much so that in Spain the term for italic in the sixteenth century and later was 'Grifo'), and of his numerous productions the most familiar are the little 12mo and 16mo volumes of Latin classics in small italic letter with his device of a griffin on the title-page. These handy pocket editions became very popular and the format was adopted by Guillaume Roville, likewise of Lyons, and by other publishers. Later the city became the centre for a school of engravers, of whom Bernard Salomon is the best known to-day. The publishing house of de Tournes practically monopolized the work of this group, and a number of very pretty illustrated books, large and small, testify to the harmonious union between cuts, arabesque borders and type which could be achieved by men of taste.

In the second half of the sixteenth century attention gravitates to the Low Countries, and especially to the Plantin press at Antwerp. Christopher Plantin was for a time a worker in fine bindings; but he afterwards returned to his original occupation of printing, and from a small beginning built up one of the largest printing houses in Europe. The extent of his business, the importance of his publications and the excellence of his workmanship brought Plantin a European reputation. The books which issued from his press cover a wide range of subjects: science, history, jurisprudence, the writings of the Fathers, Greek and Latin classics, and books in Hebrew. Many were finely illustrated, and all bear evidence of his care and taste, while his biggest undertaking, the Antwerp Polyglot Bible (1569–73), exhibits to advantage the handsome character of the types which distinguish his books. In 1570 Plantin received from Philip II a special privilege for the printing of liturgical books, and his press was soon turning out missals, breviaries, books of hours and other service books in enormous numbers. This class of book came to be a main feature in the output of the *Officina Plantiniana* and was afterwards one of the chief sources of its prosperity.

After the founder's death in 1589 the Plantin press maintained its high standard of workmanship under the direction of his son-in-law, Jean Moretus; but there was a falling off in both the volume and the importance of the output, science and classical works giving place to ecclesiastical history and books of devotion. The energetic reign (1610–41) of Balthasar Moretus, son of Jean, brought a revival of prestige; but after the death of Balthasar the second in 1674, attention was almost entirely confined to the printing of liturgical books. The business continued to be carried on by successive members of the family down to 1876, when this stately printing house was acquired by the city of Antwerp and preserved as the Musée Plantin-Moretus.

In the seventeenth century the vogue for books of diminutive size reached its zenith in the little 32mo volumes associated with the name of Elzevir, a family who for upwards of a century carried on business in Leyden, Amsterdam and other towns. In the Elzevirs we have parted company with the scholar-printers who themselves edited and revised the texts which they presented to the learned world. We have instead intelligent printer-publishers, who were primarily men of business, however anxious to produce books that both textually and typographically should sustain their credit for good work.

The origin of the house goes back to 1583, in which year Louis Elzevir, a migrant from Louvain, commenced publishing in Leyden. But it is from 1626, when Bonaventura Elzevir, a son of the founder, was joined by his nephew Abraham, that the fame of the house really begins. It was then that, having acquired a printing office of their own, they began to specialize in the issue of the characteristic small volumes, and the period from 1626 to the death of both partners in 1652 was the golden age of the firm. Bonaventura and Abraham were succeeded by their sons Jean and Daniel. In 1655 Daniel migrated to Amsterdam to join his cousin Louis, and the fortuitously celebrated *Pastissier françois* (a mere reprint of a Paris edition of 1653) bears the imprint of these two in that same year. Thenceforth the Amsterdam house took the leading place, and so continued until the death of Daniel in 1680. In all, some fifteen members of the family had been engaged in the book trade before the house came to an ignoble end at Leyden in the hands of the younger Abraham in 1712.

The small Elzevir volumes achieved great contemporary popularity, and many authors thought it an honour to have their writings included in the series. But the acclaim was punctuated here and there with complaints at the smallness of type and the loss of dignity sustained by important works in being printed in such diminutive format. The long series of volumes contained a large proportion of the classic and standard literature of the day in well-printed and fairly correct editions, and possessing the special advantage that their small size enabled them to be sold at a price (many of them were published at eighteenpence to two shillings) which brought them within easy reach of a wide circle of readers. In short, they stood in much the same relation to the ordinary edition as does the Everyman or Penguin of to-day to the seven-and-sixpenny edition. Their contemporary success is therefore not surprising; but it is not so easy to account for the great fascination they have possessed for later generations of collectors. They cannot be considered attractive books: in truth, they are scrubby little volumes, and the narrow page gives them a mean and cramped feeling. For comeliness they cannot compare with the small books issued by Simon de Colines, the Gryphii, Christopher Plantin and other sixteenth-century printers: yet a 'tall' Elzevir of the 'correct' period used to throw Dibdin into an ecstasy.

The success of the Elzevir books naturally brought imitations and even counterfeits. But the Elzevirs had little room for complaint on this score, for in that age of free trade in literature they did not scruple to add to their own series any book they thought worth inclusion, probably deeming it more of a compliment to the author's fame than any wrong done to his pocket. Among the more prominent of their rivals were Jean Maire and Frans Hacke (Hackius), two of the six-and-twenty booksellers who were carrying on business in Leyden in 1651; and in Amsterdam, Jan Jansson, Abraham Wolfgang and Jan Blaeu. The last of these, one of the principal Dutch printers of his day, is, however, more celebrated for the massive illustrated books which issued from his nine presses, each presided over by one of the Muses. It was his father, the cartographer Willem Janszoon Blaeu, who about 1620 made certain improvements* in the structure of the printing press, which up to that time had differed but little from the press of the early printers. Nor was there further change of any moment until, at the end of the eighteenth century, Earl Stanhope constructed, in England, the first iron printing press.

* Improvements highly praised, but very imperfectly explained, by the historian Joseph Moxon.

CHAPTER V

ENGLISH BOOKS, 1500–1800

In the early years of the sixteenth century Wynkyn de Worde and Richard Pynson were the chief printers in England. The volume of printing going on in the country since its introduction by Caxton was slowly increasing, and fresh presses were being set up. The more prominent names include Robert Copland, a printer of literary tastes; John Rastell, a printer of law books; and Thomas Berthelet, who on the death of Pynson in 1530 succeeded to the office of King's Printer. The books which came from the native press continued to be of a strictly insular character, and very few of them could have appealed to readers across the Channel. It was still found more profitable to import books from the continent than to reprint them here; and some of the foreign printers were now printing books specially for the English market. The majority of these books were liturgical works of English use, and until they were displaced in the reign of Henry VIII, a large trade in them was carried on, mostly by French printers. Chief among these were Antoine Vérard and François Regnault of Paris, the latter of whom had also a book shop in London. In 1538, an edition of Coverdale's version of the Bible which Regnault was printing was seized and publicly burned in Paris. Jan van Doesborch catered for a different public when he printed at Antwerp, between 1508 and 1530, *Tyll Howleglas*, *Robin Hood*, and other popular English stories: but for a hundred years after the middle of the century most of the books printed abroad for sale in England were concerned with religious and political controversy and had to be imported and circulated surreptitiously.

The most important event of the sixteenth century affecting the production of books in England was the incorporation of the Stationers' Company in 1557. Under the charter of incorporation no one was permitted to print anything for sale unless he were a member of the Company; and every member was required to enter in the Company's register the name of any book or 'copy' which he claimed as his property and desired to print. The craft of printing was thus strictly organized, and a supervision inaugurated which was to exercise an important influence upon the production and distribution of books for the next hundred and fifty years.

As printing increased and the power of the press as an instrument for the dissemination of ideas and opinions became more evident, both church and state developed a desire to control the output of printed matter. The Stationers' Company, with its charter powers, was regarded as a convenient agent for the exercise of such control, and from the middle of the sixteenth to the end of the seventeenth century the press was subjected to continual attempts to regulate it in accordance with the views of those in authority for the time being.

At the very beginning of Elizabeth's reign a system of censorship was introduced by an injunction ordering that no book should be printed unless it were first licensed by certain authorities. This regulation being indifferently observed, other orders followed, and in 1586 the Star Chamber issued a stringent decree for the regulation of printing. This decree gave the authorities a more effective hold upon the legitimate press, but the suppression of seditious and heretical books, many of which were printed abroad and imported surreptitiously, was far from being successfully achieved.

Before the Stationers' Company received its charter, printing had been carried on at Oxford, St Albans, York, Cambridge, Tavistock, Abingdon, Ipswich, Worcester and Canterbury. By 1557 all these presses were extinct, and with one trifling exception no printing was done outside London until the Cambridge press was revived by the University in 1583. A similar revival followed at Oxford two years later. In 1586 there were in London twenty-five master printers, owning among them fifty-three presses; and since the Star Chamber decree of that year permitted no addition to these numbers, the production of books was limited to the capacity of the existing presses.

Notwithstanding official restrictions, the literary activity of the Elizabethan era was accompanied by an enormous increase in the output of the press. New poems, new plays, translations from other literatures, especially Latin, French and Italian, followed each other in quick procession, varied by graver treatises such as chronicles, voyages and travels, philosophical dissertations and works of theology. All these were in addition to numberless Bibles, prayer-books, legal treatises, and A B C's and other school books, which, though more prosaic, brought much profit to those printers who were fortunate enough to possess these monopolies.

Altogether the period covered by the reigns of Elizabeth and James I is one of the most prolific in the whole story of book production in England.

The list of English printers of this period contains no names which can stand beside their great continental contemporaries; but some respectable work was done by the best native presses, and enterprise and taste are apparent in some of the more important publications. Richard Grafton and Edward Whitchurch printed several issues of the *Book of Common Prayer* in the reign of Edward VI. Besides printing Hardyng's *Chronicle of Englande* and kindred works, Grafton also compiled two historical chronicles, which were printed by his son-in-law Richard Tottell in 1562 and 1569. This Tottell, publisher of the well-known poetical *Miscellany* which goes under his name, was the owner of an exclusive patent for the printing of law books. Henry Debenham displayed good taste in many of the books he printed between 1564 and 1589; and Richard Jugge, four times master of the Stationers' Company, issued in 1568 the first edition of the 'Bishops' Bible', a fine book containing good copper-plate portraits. From a typographical point of view the outstanding name is John Day, whose career extended from 1546 to 1584. Under the patronage of Archbishop Parker, that Maecenas of art and letters, Day had several new founts of type cut, and his work lifted English printing to a higher level. The first book printed in Anglo-Saxon characters (Aelfric's *Paschal Homily*) came from his press, as did also the English version of Foxe's *Book of Martyrs* (1563). It is probable that for a time Foxe himself worked in some editorial capacity in Day's printing house, as he had previously done at Basel in the office of Oporinus, who published the first (Latin) edition of his famous book in 1559.

The most influential man in the Company at this time was Christopher Barker, who as Queen's Printer was much occupied with Bibles and official work. He was succeeded in 1599 by his son Robert, publisher of the King James Version (the 'Authorized Version') of the Bible in 1611. Another important stationer was William Ponsonby, the leading literary publisher of Elizabethan times. In 1590 he brought out Sir Philip Sidney's *Arcadia*, and in the same year the first three books of Spenser's *Faerie Queene*. Edward Blount, who succeeded to Ponsonby's place as a publisher of *belles lettres*, issued in 1603 Florio's translation of Montaigne's *Essays*, and published several of Marlowe's works. He was also one of the four partners in the publication of the First Folio *Shakespeare* (1623). John Norton was in a big way of business, and his name is borne by some of the most important books of the first decade of the seventeenth century. George Bishop, another prominent man, was partner in Holinshed's *Chronicles* and Hakluyt's *Voyages*; and John Bill, publisher of Bacon's *Instauratio Magna*, was bookseller to King James and Sir Thomas Bodley.

But none of these names are to be found in the imprints of one of the most interesting sections of Elizabethan literature—those precious, thin, ill-printed quartos in which the plays of Shakespeare and his fellow dramatists made their first appearance in print. These, hardly worthy the notice of big publishers and opulent monopolists, were left to the more obscure men, who have little else to distinguish them among the eight hundred and more Londoners who, between 1540 and 1640, engaged in the printing and selling of books. Among those who were concerned with the Shakespeare quartos were John Busby, Andrew Wise, Edward White, a dealer in ballads, James Roberts, the almanac patentee, and John Danter, an unscrupulous pirate.

Having regard to the comparatively small field open to English printers of the sixteenth century, and the official restrictions and vexations to which they were subjected, we need not be surprised that printing in this country did not attain any great degree of excellence. But, apart from technical merit, the production of the great body of Elizabethan literature from the small number of existing presses is a sufficiently noteworthy performance. It must be remembered, however, that many of the larger undertakings, such as the folio editions of Shakespeare or of Beaumont and Fletcher, were divided up between several printing houses, each of which was responsible for a different section of the complete book. Even substantial firms would otherwise have been hampered in their work by the 'locking up' of such a large quantity of type.

Up to the middle of the century English books retain much of their early character, but by about 1580 roman type had come into general use, displacing the old black letter for almost all books except Bibles, law books and a few other special classes. Italic letter was also used to a considerable extent, but chiefly in a subsidiary capacity, and it never in England acquired the vogue it had attained on the continent as a text type. Throughout the sixteenth century a border was a common adornment of the title-page, and the wording of the title was usually fairly brief and simple. These borders were of various kinds, architectural and arabesque ornament predominating; and in the second half of the century an effective border built up with combinations of small flowers was frequently employed. Titles in the Stuart period tend to become verbose, for copies were often struck off as single leaves for the purpose of advertising the book. The border, for which there is no longer room, disappears; and the title sprawls down the page in a confused variety of types. In controversial works the title-page sometimes affords an opening for a telling home-thrust at an adversary; allusive titles, which give no indication of the subject-matter of the book, are frequent; while the lure of alliteration was too seldom resisted by the writers of pious tractates.

From the accession of Charles I the censorship of literature, which had relaxed somewhat in the previous reign, was exercised with fresh vigour; but on the abolition of the Star Chamber in 1641 all restraint vanished for the time being, and by 1649 the number of printing houses in London had increased to more than sixty. The main occupation of these presses was the printing of pamphlets. The Civil War was a conflict of words and arguments as well as of arms, and whole regiments of pamphlets were pressed into the service on each side, charge and counter-charge making a clash and din amid which literature itself was wellnigh shouted down. The Parliamentary party, although professed champions of liberty, found this freedom little to their taste. They soon endeavoured to put a curb upon the press, and it was their action that called forth

Milton's eloquent plea for the liberty of unlicensed printing. But the *Areopagitica* (1644) fell upon deaf ears, and the news press at least continued to be the object of a strict censorship.

Above the flood of pamphlets a few books stand out like landmarks, preserving the continuity of letters through this stressful period. Sir Thomas Browne's *Religio Medici* made its unauthorized appearance in 1642, and in 1645 Milton's collected poems were brought out by Humphrey Moseley, the publisher of Lovelace, Crashaw, Suckling, Herrick and other poets. In 1650 came Jeremy Taylor's *Holy Living*, followed the next year by his *Holy Dying*; and the first edition of Izaak Walton's *Compleat Angler* was published in 1653. There were also larger books, like the first volume of Dugdale's *Monasticon Anglicanum* (1655); and that *tour de force* of the English seventeenth-century press, Brian Walton's Polyglot Bible, which contains the text of the Scriptures in nine languages and was printed by Thomas Roycroft in six folio volumes in 1654–7.

In the more settled times of the Restoration literature experienced a revival. This revival was accompanied by a resuscitation of the censorship, and the Licensing Act of 1662, as administered by that active zealot Roger L'Estrange, was the most stringent measure of press control ever put into force in this country. This act, after being renewed at intervals, finally expired in 1694, and no further attempt was made to supervise the output of the press. Among the books of this time theology holds a largely preponderating place, particularly that section of it usually termed practical divinity, such as the writings of Richard Baxter and John Bunyan, and the sermons of South and Tillotson. Indeed the *Pilgrim's Progress*, which made its first appearance in 1678, is more typical of the books in common circulation at that time than, say, Wycherley's play *The Plain Dealer*, published in the preceding year. Dramatists, nevertheless, were prolific as well as distinguished; and the pamphlet, though now occupying a less prominent position, was still much used as a vehicle for the expression of political and other controversial opinion.

With the opening of the eighteenth century the world of books begins to approach modern conditions. The habit of reading was no longer confined to the limited circle of the learned and the leisured, and literature was now addressing itself to the people at large. *The Tatler* of 1709–11 was succeeded by *The Spectator* of 1711–12, which circulated in thousands and had many imitators and successors. *Robinson Crusoe* made its debut in 1719, *Gulliver's Travels* in 1726, and the *Gentleman's Magazine* was launched by Edward Cave in 1731. Richardson's *Pamela*, which appeared in 1741, was followed two years later by Fielding's *Joseph Andrews*. After these came *Clarissa Harlowe* (1747–8), Smollett's *Roderick Random* (1748), *Tom Jones* (1749); and the novel from now on occupies an increasingly prominent position in the world of books. The remarkable literary activity of this century is also noticeable in other directions. Up to 1709 the collected works of Shakespeare were accessible only in the four folio editions of 1623, 1632, 1664 and 1685; but between 1709 and 1790 there were published upwards of twenty critical editions. The impressive labours of Hume, Robertson and Gibbon inaugurated a new era in historical study; and the numerous works dealing with local history and antiquities gave occasion for the production of some fine books illustrated with engravings. At the other end of the scale are the children's books, *Tommy Prudent*, *Goody Two Shoes*, and other 'improving' stories, which have rendered famous their publisher and originator, John Newbery, the busy bookseller and patent-medicine vendor of St Paul's Churchyard.

The right of an author to property in his work was recognized for the first time by the law of the land in the Copyright Act of 1709. As a rule, however, authors continued to sell their work outright to publishers, and in the eighteenth century the professional writer was to a great extent the employee of the bookseller-publisher. The leading publisher at the opening of the century was Jacob Tonson of the 'Shakespear Head', who published for Dryden. A little later came Bernard Lintot, whose name is connected with that of Pope. Robert Dodsley, himself a poet and playwright, published works by Samuel Johnson, Gray, Goldsmith, and others of his large circle of friends. The energetic Andrew Millar carried through the arrangements for bringing out Johnson's *Dictionary* (1755), and his successors Thomas Cadell and William Strahan were in their turn important personages in the publishing world.

For two hundred years the ordinary sizes for English books had continued to be the folio, measuring about 12 by 7½ inches, and the quarto, of about 7½ by 6 inches—both smaller than the sizes we understand by these terms to-day. The two main sizes were varied by a larger folio for more important works, and an octavo about 6 inches high for the smaller books. In the eighteenth century there is a greater variety of sizes and a larger paper is in general use. The folio is still used, more especially for topographical works with illustrations, but for 'general' books and the more prosperous poetry it gives way to the quarto: not the small square book of the preceding century, but a more imposing volume, measuring some 10 by 8 inches, in which there is space, as occasion may demand, either for packing much matter, or for the luxury of large type and wide margins. For everyday literature the convenient octavo size and also a large duodecimo (7 by 4 inches) came into general use. The standard of printing as a whole shows a considerable improvement upon the dark days of the Commonwealth period, though with some exceptions the craftsmanship is still mediocre and the appearance of the books undistinguished. In general, the paper is indifferent in quality and too brown in colour, while the ink lacks sufficient blackness to make a good contrast; and this gives an appearance of weakness to the printed page, which was tacitly admitted by the frequency of the superior (and much dearer) issue on special, usually Dutch, paper.

During the first quarter of the eighteenth century and for some time previously most of the best type in use in England came from Holland, the country which at that time held pride of place in the printing world. When Richard Bentley was reorganizing the University Press at Cambridge towards the end of the seventeenth century, it was to Holland that he sent for new type, and a Dutchman, Cornelius Crownfield, was engaged to superintend the work. Dutch too were the models employed when in 1667 Dr John Fell established a type-

THE

Hiſtory of the Rebellion, &c.

BOOK XVI.

Zechar. II. 4, 5, 6.

Thus ſaith the Lord my God, Feed the flock of the ſlaughter.
Whoſe poſſeſſors ſlay them, and hold themſelves not guilty: and they that ſell them, ſay, Bleſſed be the Lord, for I am rich: and their own ſhepherds pity them not.
-----But lo, I will deliver the men every one into his Neighbours hand, and into the hand of his King.

The beginning of Richard's Government.

CONTRARY to all expectation both at home and abroad, this Earthquake was attended with no ſignal Alteration. It was believ'd that *Lambert* would be in the head of the Army, and that *Monk* in *Scotland* would never ſubmit to be under him. Beſides the expectation the King had from the general Affection of the Kingdom, he had fair promiſes from Men of Intereſt in it, and of Command in the Army, who profeſſed to prepare for ſuch a Conjuncture as this; and that the diſorder ariſing from *Cromwell*'s death might diſpoſe *Lockhart* to depend upon the beſt Title, ſeem'd a reaſonable expectation: but nothing of this fell out. Never Monarch, after he had inherited a Crown by many deſcents, died in more ſilence, nor with leſs alteration; and there was the ſame, or a greater calm in the Kingdom than had been before.

THE next morning after the death of *Oliver*, *Richard* his Son is proclaim'd his Lawful Succeſſor; the Army congratulate their new General, and renew their Vows of fidelity to him; the Navy doth the like; the City appears more unanimous for His Service, than they were for his Father's; and moſt Counties in *England*, by Addreſſes under their hands, teſtified their obedience to their new Soveraign without any heſitation. The dead is interr'd in the Sepulcher of the Kings, and with the obſequies due to ſuch. His Son inherits all his Greatneſs, and all his

Page from Clarendon's *History of the Rebellion* (Oxford, 1702–4)

XII.

On leaving some Friends at an early Hour.

GIVE me a golden pen, and let me lean
On heap'd up flowers, in regions clear, and far;
Bring me a tablet whiter than a star,
Or hand of hymning angel, when 'tis seen
The silver strings of heavenly harp atween:
And let there glide by many a pearly car,
Pink robes, and wavy hair, and diamond jar,
And half discovered wings, and glances keen.
The while let music wander round my ears,
And as it reaches each delicious ending,
Let me write down a line of glorious tone,
And full of many wonders of the spheres:
For what a height my spirit is contending!
'Tis not content so soon to be alone.

Page from Keats's *Poems* (London, 1817)

foundry for the Oxford University Press, and for several years afterwards some of the best printing in this country was done at Oxford. Good examples may be seen in Anthony Wood's *Historia Universitatis Oxoniensis* (1674) and George Hickes's *Thesaurus* (1705), which came from the University Press, and the magnificent Bible printed by John Baskett in 1716–17, which, however, from the numerous misprints it contains, came to be known as 'a Baskett-full of printer's errors'. Other efforts to improve English typography were being made, and in 1722 William Caslon, who had experimented in type-cutting, designed for William Bowyer, an excellent printer, a new and handsome fount of roman and italic letter which was used for the folio edition of Selden's works printed in 1726. The beauty of the Caslon letter soon brought it into favour, and though it was for a considerable period eclipsed by the 'modern style' types made fashionable by Baskerville and the Didots, it has been revived and it remains one of the soundest faces ever cast in any country.

Printing had now spread throughout the provinces, and every town of importance could boast its printing press. The greater number of these presses were connected with the publication of newspapers, and few places produced books of any note. An outstanding exception is the work of John Baskerville at Birmingham. Baskerville, who was a skilled penman and cutter of monumental inscriptions, turned his attention to type-founding, and issued in 1757 a quarto edition of Virgil as his first book. This was followed by a Milton; other Latin classics in quarto; several Prayer Books and a folio Bible, printed for the University of Cambridge;

and a number of miscellaneous works. Baskerville's was the first consciously 'fine printing' in England, and his contemporary reputation was higher abroad than at home. His business was not a commercial success, and his types made little headway in the trade at the time, though their posthumous influence was considerable. Later historians have bracketed his name with those of his illustrious contemporaries, Bodoni of Parma and the Didots of Paris; indeed, his influence on these printers was strong and Bodoni was one of several continental printers to acknowledge the debt. Baskerville must, above all, always be honoured for his recognition of the importance in good printing of a high quality in both ink and paper.

The aim which the brothers Robert and Andrew Foulis set before themselves when they established their famous press in Glasgow was not merely to bring out well-printed books. They aspired also to the distinction of a learned press; and both the quality of their printing and the accuracy of their texts give them a claim to be classed with the scholar-printers of the sixteenth century. Greek and Latin classics and reprints of standard works form the bulk of the numerous publications, more than 550 in number, which they issued between 1742 and 1776. Among these the great *Homer* of 1756–8, in four folio volumes, stands out pre-eminent, and shows to advantage their simplified fount of Greek type. This is significant as the first serious revulsion from that heavily ligatured manner which was the evil legacy of Aldus: a manner only finally shed by the 'Great Porson Greek' introduced by the Cambridge University Press in the 1820's. Foulis's renowned 'immaculate' *Horace* of 1744, with only six errors, is one of the many volumes in smaller format, the good printing, careful editing and moderate price of which are characteristic of their press.

The stately volumes printed by Thomas Bensley and by William Bulmer in the closing years of the eighteenth century should perhaps be regarded as first-fruits of Baskerville's influence on the modern period of printing: but this chapter cannot be concluded without reference to the man who, more than any other single person, gave that modern period its impetus and its character; namely, John Bell. Bell was ahead of his time as a newspaper proprietor, as a publisher, and last, but for us most important, as a typographer. It is to him, for instance, that we attribute the abolition of the long 's'. His skilful combination of elegance and novelty with sound design not only exerted a profound influence on the format of the book, but also established, through his type-designs, the temporary supremacy and permanent adoption of modern style type in England.

CHAPTER VI

THE MODERN BOOK

Until the beginning of the nineteenth century there was little printing apart from books, and what there was clung closely to bookish traditions. But now, with the widening field of the 'jobbing' printer and the development by Robert Thorne and others of 'grotesque' types which were only suitable for display work, a cleavage appears. The jobbing printer's work clearly offers greater incentives to originality; indeed, his success depends on it. We are not surprised, therefore, in the years which follow, to find a greater share of inventiveness and skill applied to that side of the art of printing than to the production of books.

This, however, was not the only, or indeed the foremost reason, for the artistic decline of the book in the nineteenth century. The influx of wealth into England as a result of mechanization, and the opportunities for virtuosity which that mechanization offered, created a taste for the ornate and specious which shows itself in the books of the time no less than in other industrial arts. At the same time, poor wages and conditions fostered abuses, such as carelessness in typographical detail and the wide spacing of words to make more lines and pages, a practice even encouraged by certain publishers for the protraction of three-volume novels. Low as the quality of printing became, however, the quantity rose continuously. In the history of the book in this century it is the publisher rather than the printer who takes pride of place.

As for printers only three names stand out with any prominence until we reach the nineties—Bulmer, Bensley and Whittingham; and of these Bulmer and Bensley had done their best work before the century began. Nevertheless, for the first thirty years the general standard of printing throughout England was higher than ever before. The 'modern' types which were exclusively used have since fallen in popularity, owing to their severity and the tiring contrast of their thick and thin strokes; but in certain varieties and in certain sizes they are not unpleasant to read, and their vitality and sparkle at least stimulated printers to provide them with the clean presswork and crisp white paper that they needed to show them off. Wide spacing of the lines was also a general rule. In all these points we may detect the lasting influence of Baskerville and his continental contemporaries, Bodoni and the Didots.

Of the few conspicuous books of this period, mention may be made of Ackermann's *Microcosm of London*, mostly remarkable for its illustrations by Pugin and Rowlandson; the imposing Boydell *Shakespeare* completed by Bulmer in 1802; Dibdin's *Bibliographical Decameron* (1817), also from Bulmer's press; and abroad, the Louvre edition of Racine printed by Pierre Didot (1801–5), a conspicuous example of the neo-classical style, and the issue of Bodoni's complete *Manuale Tipografico* in 1818, five years after his death.

Unexciting as these years were in the realm of books, they were markedly important in the technical side of printing history. The earliest power-driven press was invented by Frederick Koenig in 1811 with the help and encouragement of Bensley and was used for printing a portion of the *Annual Register*. The following year witnessed Koenig's invention of the first cylinder machine. It was successfully used for a portion of Clarkson's *Life of Penn* and was at once adopted by *The Times* newspaper. With the backing of that journal and its resources, the speed of printing rose with a leap from 250 to 1000 impressions an hour, and it was to be expected that newspapers, for which speed of production is of first importance, should provide the main incentive for further developments in this direction. The first press devised for printing from continuous reels of paper was produced in America in 1865, a year or two before *The Times* patented the Walter press, the output of which amounted to fifteen thousand completed copies of the newspaper in an hour.

Printing from continuous reels would have been impracticable without the help of stereotyping, which was invented by an Edinburgh goldsmith, William Ged, in 1727 and shortly afterwards commercialized for the production of Bibles and prayer-books at the Cambridge Press. By this process a mould is taken of the type-page in damp papier-mâché. The mould is then baked hard and molten metal is poured into it which, upon cooling, forms a solid plate exactly reproducing the original type. Stereotyping is widely used to-day for books of which numerous impressions are likely to be wanted, the original moulds being preserved for further castings should one set of plates prove insufficient. Ged, however, had little success with his invention, and the art fell into disuse after his death, until Earl Stanhope, the resourceful inventor of the iron printing press, revived it about 1800. The device of bending the mould and casting a curved plate, which could then be clamped to a cylinder, was an essential adjunct to John Walter's rotary press, the principle of which was the synchronized revolution of pairs of cylinders, one carrying the inked plate, the other providing the pressure as the paper passed between.

Reel-printing is unsuitable for books, partly because it entails the expense of stereotyping even for short runs, partly because of the restriction of size imposed by the plate cylinder. Flat-bed machines are normally used for books, a heavy cylinder providing the pressure as the type is carried on a sliding bed beneath it, and the paper being fed in, automatically or by hand, in single sheets. The motion is, of course, much slower, since half the time is taken up with the backward travel of the bed, and the constant change of direction sets a heavy strain on the machine if carried out too rapidly. Nevertheless, the speed of these machines has risen considerably in recent years.

The production of paper by machine was invented in France by Nicholas Louis Robert in the last years of the eighteenth century, and was developed in England by Henry and Sealy Fourdrinier. In 1809 John Dickinson's cylinder machine carried the process still further. The consequences of this invention were far-reaching; not only did paper become cheaper to manufacture, but it could also be supplied in much larger sheets than the old hand-mould could contain. The available supplies of rag and cotton, however, were not sufficient for the steadily increasing demand, and numerous experiments with such fibrous substances as straw, wood, nettles, marsh mallow, and even moss, proved of little value so far as printing papers were concerned. In 1854 *The Times* added an incentive to research with an offer of £1000 for an efficient substitute for cotton, and at last, in 1861, the year of the repeal of the Paper Duty, the manufacture of paper from the fibres of esparto grass was successfully commercialized. Wood-pulp, which forms the other staple material to-day, was first prepared in Germany in the forties by mechanical grinding, but only inferior qualities of paper are obtainable through this method. Chemical means of separating the fibres, first the soda or alkali process and later the sulphite or acid process, were found to preserve them in purer and more lasting state, and by the eighties these methods were in general use.

The technical advances of the first quarter of the century and the increasing size of the reading public combined to produce during the opening years of the second a crop of books which were not only indicative of the trend of the time but also markedly influential on the book production of the succeeding decades. Constable's *Miscellany*, Murray's *Family Library*, the Cadell cheap collected edition of Scott, Lardner's *Cabinet Cyclopaedia* and similar series led the way; while Knight's *Library of Entertaining Knowledge* and Bentley's *Standard Novels* drove home the lesson, that topical reprints and original instruction could be cheap and saleable and at the same time shapely, solid, well-made books. The excellent results obtained by Murray, Macrone, Blackwood and other progressive publishers of the period would not have been possible without Stanhope and

Koenig, Leighton and the Imperial Arming Press: but equally the inventors' efforts would not have flowered so bravely on the reader's table without the lively encouragement of publishing enterprise. The thirties and early forties, in fact, produced some of the best-looking ordinary commercial books of the whole nineteenth century, even if they were not the most distinguished from a purely typographical point of view.

The sensational success of *The Pickwick Papers* in 1837 introduced a new development of an established form of publishing, and one which for a time seriously challenged the impregnable position of the three-decker in the fiction market: namely, the part issue. These large octavo paper-covered issues were aimed at the buyer, as opposed to the borrower, of novels. The serial parts were published, usually monthly, at a shilling: they were illustrated by some popular artist; and the complete set (running from 12 to 20) was ultimately put into a binding case supplied by the publisher. Dickens, Ainsworth, Thackeray, Trollope, Surtees and Lever all appeared regularly 'in parts'. The part issue continued as a popular and successful medium for fiction for three decades: but it was only adapted to 'best-selling' authors, such as those mentioned, since long printings were economically necessary; and the majority of novelists continued chained to the circulating library and its Procrustean bed—the three-volume format.

A contrast to the good sense and good taste of the thirties and a foretaste of what was to come was provided by an extraordinary outburst, during the forties, from the usually staid firm of Longman. Utilizing, and perhaps inspired by, the colourful elaborations of Owen

Jones and Noel Humphreys, they put out a number of books, mostly reprints, with gilt and illuminated title-pages, lavish textual bordering in dizzy colours, and bindings of Dutch paper, stamped leatherwork, or incised papier-mâché. This riot of fancy was short-lived, and it had little visible effect on contemporary style, which remained till the middle fifties uninspired in typography if decent as to exterior. Exceptions were provided by the always admirable but somewhat archaistic Pickering, and occasionally others: but the lively marbled and spotted and striped binding cloths which were popular between 1850 and the early sixties were seldom combined with any but dismal text layouts.

The revival of the Caslon letter in the forties was one of the landmarks in the history of English printing, and broke the established practice of half a century. The book usually associated with its rebirth is *Lady Willoughby's Diary* printed by the younger Whittingham for Messrs Longman in 1844, but in fact it had found occasional use for some years before, as in the antiquarian reprints which Whittingham printed for Pickering. With obvious relief, publishers and printers abandoned the restraint imposed by the 'modern' types, with results that were mainly disastrous. Pages were frequently surrounded by frames and encrusted with ornamental head and tail pieces and elaborate initials, and a profusion of sentimental wood-cut vignettes. The quality of paper deteriorated, and type-faces of weak and mechanical design were introduced, a poor tribute to Caslon's fine letter which they were considered to improve.

Of the familiar illustrated 'table-books', mostly poetical, which are usually associated with 'the Sixties', a few, such as the *Tennyson* of 1857, Dalziel's *Arabian Nights*, or Thornbury's *Legendary Ballads* of 1876, have real pictorial beauty; but the majority seem to-day wishywashy in design and feeling, even if technically accomplished. And their ornate bindings similarly contrast first-class workmanship with a meaningless elaboration of pattern. Alongside these, however, the stream of serious contemporary verse pursued the physically sober course charted by Edward Moxon, inheritor of the tradition of Taylor and Hessey and Effingham Wilson, and still visible in the poetical format affected by Strahan, Smith Elder and Macmillan in the seventies. Yet the decline in ordinary trade printing can be measured, all the more plainly for their family likeness, by a comparison of Keats's *Poems* (1817) with *In Memoriam* (1850), *Ionica* (1858) or *The Ring and the Book* (1868).

The format of general literature after 1850 became more and more undistinguished, with relief again appearing only occasionally in the binding. But against this sad-looking background the pictorially boarded cheap series commonly known as 'yellow-backs' provided an ever more riotous show of fanciful design and gaudy colours. Their cheap paper, shoddy layout and vile presswork must have made them trying reading for those railway journeys to which many of them were nominally dedicated. But the skill of Edmund Evans's colour printing and the lively variety of the artists employed gave welcome play to that comfortable, engaging, romantic vulgarity which leavened the Victorians' devotion to Tupper, Smiles and Mrs Humphry Ward.

Typographically, however, it must be admitted that there are few redeeming exceptions to the general decline of standards and of taste until the first (and perhaps best) work of William Morris begins to appear in the books which he designed for Ellis and White in the late sixties and the seventies. The Pre-Raphaelites had left their mark on book production, as the volumes of the Rossettis, and one or two of Swinburne, show: but Morris struck immediately a robuster though still self-conscious note. At Oxford Henry Daniel revived the seventeenth-century Fell types for use in a series of limited editions of considerable charm, and the eighties saw the production in London of two finely printed magazines, *The Hobby Horse* of Herbert Horne and Selwyn Image, and *The Dial* of Hacon and Ricketts. A revival of printing seemed to be on the way, though hardly less archaistic in spirit than Whittingham's deliberate expedition into the sixteenth century. The books which started to issue from the Kelmscott Press at Hammersmith in 1891, and which were to have so much influence here and abroad, went back for their inspiration to the very beginnings of printing.

Morris's aim in founding his press was to rescue the art of printing from the mechanical dreariness into which it had lapsed. With the collaboration of Emery Walker he produced between 1891 and 1897 fifty-three books of monumental richness, beautifully printed in specially designed types on hand-made paper, bound in flawless vellum or in blue-papered boards with holland back, and usually limited to 250 or fewer copies. Their painstaking composition, exquisite presswork, and harmonious decoration by Burne-Jones and others, set an example which had lasting and healthy effect in many countries. On the other hand, his use of period types, based on the earliest Italian models, and his lack of concern for legibility, had evil consequences which lasted for twenty years after his death. And his patronage of old hand-methods did nothing to help machinery in its struggling days of self-discovery.

A galaxy of other private presses arose—Doves, Ashendene, Eragny, Essex House, Vale—to emulate Morris in producing 'the book beautiful'. The Ashendene, which produced its last volume (a descriptive bibliography of its work) in 1935, was the only one of these to attain a ripe age, and its *Dante* ranks with the Kelmscott *Chaucer* and the Doves *Bible* as one of the outstanding and highly prized volumes of this conspicuous movement in fine printing. A few other private presses, based on the Kelmscott model, have since been established, providing artists and craftsmen with opportunities for the exercise of their skill. But historically they are no longer important. The commercial printer of to-day has learned his lesson, indirectly but no less effectively, from Morris and his followers, and exploits all the possibilities of good printing without need of further stimulus of this particular kind.

The countries which benefited most from Morris's work were England, Germany and the United States. All three had previously shown some reawakening of typographical interest, so that the seed fell on fertile ground. In Germany, where the variety of letter forms gives livelihood to an exceptional number of typefounders, good work in fresh type-design was being carried on in the eighties, and in 1895 a conspicuous piece of printing appeared in the periodical *Pan*, supported by a group of young artists and writers led by Meier Graefe and printed by the Leipzig firm of Drugulin. Admiration of the private press movement in England led to a number of imitators, such as Count Kessler, who produced from his press at Weimar a number of fine books on the Doves model. In America, Theodore De Vinne, Walter Gillis, and D. B. Updike worked, not without success, to infuse into books a degree of taste and personality. Some of the latter's early work at the Merrymount Press, which he founded in 1893, reflects the Morris influence, but he was too good a scholar, too original an artist and too enterprising a craftsman to limit himself within any narrow or derived style.

While Morris was hammering out his magnificent tomes at the Kelmscott Press, another but very different movement towards good printing was astir in England, fostered by Elkin Mathews and John Lane of the Bodley Head. Its aim was similar to Morris's—to rescue the book from mechanical degeneration by putting the artist in command; but its approach was widely different. Its main features were an original use of the old style types of the period, great variety in the size and shape of books, and a fruitful employment of such artists as Aubrey Beardsley, Charles Ricketts, Laurence Housman, Herbert Horne and Selwyn Image to decorate and illustrate their books with a sensitive respect for typographical discipline. The Wilde scandal discredited for a time all the writers and artists associated with him, but John Lane, Heinemann, and later Martin Secker, were three London publishers who continued to produce books of the same restrained and graceful calibre, most of them printed by the Ballantyne Press of London and Edinburgh or the firm of T. and A. Constable of Edinburgh.

Meanwhile, at the Riverside Press in America, Bruce Rogers was pursuing an individual line, which was to lead the way to the best typographical practice of to-day. An artist himself, he possessed a keen appreciation of good letter forms and printer's ornaments, which he combined with a scrupulous concern for every detail of ink, paper, presswork, colour, binding and all else that goes to make a perfect book. But his most important quality was a profound sense of the fit presentation of each particular volume he designed. Though his books are recognizable to the connoisseur, largely because of their thoroughness, there is no monotony about them. Each is penetratingly thought out and impeccably executed, and he paved the way for the large number of free-lance typographers and book-designers now flourishing in the United States.

In 1916 Bruce Rogers came to England as typographical consultant to the Cambridge Press, and has since executed several remarkable books on successive visits to this country, notably the Oxford Lectern Bible of 1935. At Cambridge he was succeeded by Stanley Morison, who was also consultant to the Monotype Corporation and responsible for much of the valuable work performed by that company in providing modern printers with beautiful and effective type-faces, some based on the best models of the past, others on the designs of living artists such as Rogers himself, Frederic Goudy, and Eric Gill.

The University Presses at Oxford and Cambridge have been responsible for much of the best printing produced since 1918, while several other publishers and printers have contributed to the large volume of good work executed in late years. Notable among recent books are those of the Nonesuch Press, planned and designed with adventurous skill by Francis Meynell. The Nonesuch aims have been the best aesthetic use of the great variety of type-faces now available and the best economic use of machines; and to combine with these a search for good paper, binding and illustration. The result has been over a hundred books of great typographical merit, astonishing variety and by no means exorbitant cost.

To summarize the state of the printed book in the world to-day is not easy. In almost all countries there is a tendency to be insular, developing at its best (as in Sweden and Czechoslovakia) into a rich nationalist movement, but at its worst restricting progress. The books of England and America, it must be admitted, are still strongly archaistic. This may be due to lack of modern type-designs suitable for books, so that the typographer is forced to use old types and make of them what he can. But deeper than this no doubt lies a widespread reluctance to turn sentimental eyes away from the past and accept the hard, mechanical present. It was republican Germany which in the years following 1918 boldly faced the fact that to deny modern man his proper typographical expression might have disastrous results, and from the Bauhaus at Dessau there suddenly issued the 'new typography', in which ornament was eschewed, types of the barest form were employed, the design of 'suspense' replaced the rectangular arrangements of the past. The early examples of this new and striking technique were crude, and it had scarcely found its way into books before reactionary political elements drove it from the country. A few English and American books, however, conceived in the style, show promising development, and we may yet see its effects spread widely. Nevertheless, an age of prosperity, or great technical advances, are required to emancipate book printing from the economic stringency which at present hinders its most useful and beautiful use.

CHAPTER VII

THE CONSTRUCTION OF A BOOK

In the construction of a book various matters must be considered: the process or processes to be used; the quality of paper; the illustrations, if any; the number of copies to be printed; the binding and jacket; and at all stages the cost, particularly in relation to the publishing price if the book is to be offered for sale. These various points are interdependent, affecting each other in many ways. In practice, however, it is unusual for them all to be settled at the outset. Although a book's final appearance may be roughly visualized at an early stage, and all the details of its production may be the concern of one person, it is often found that the preparing of illustrations is best left until the type is set, so that their arrangement and proportions may be more delicately worked out. Similarly, the final choice of paper may be postponed until the book is complete in proof form, and the design of binding and jacket until a later stage. Books tend to grow, in fact, under the constant thought and supervision of their designers.

If there are any illustrations to be included, it is on them that the choice of process chiefly depends. It may be that the lithographic or gravure methods are best suited to their nature or to the economics of their production, and that, as a result, it is desirable to print the whole book by these means. More commonly, however, we find the text printed by ordinary letter-press methods, and the illustrations by this or any of the other processes available, according to the particular circumstances. Photographic methods of composition, by which plates are prepared for lithographic printing and metal type is dispensed with, are still in their infancy and it is difficult to foretell what progress they will make. In any case, they do not affect our investigation into the stages of book production, nor the final appearance of the book except for a marked inferiority in the sharpness and blackness of the type when compared with the results of the older method.*

The next question, then, is what shall be the format of the book. Many considerations go to the settling of this important point: the use to which the book is to be put, the subject-matter, the extent of the manuscript, the demands of the illustrations. Paper-makers traditionally keep to certain sizes of sheet for their stock lines, and since the printer's machines and equipment usually conform to the same standards, it is found most convenient and economical to design books in corresponding dimensions. Happily, however, the attractions of standardization are not allowed to override altogether the important considerations of sense and freshness.

Books are not printed a page at a time, but in sheets of several pages, imposed in such a way that they run consecutively when the sheet is folded. The commoner sizes of sheets, with the measurements reached by folding them once, twice, and three times, are shown in inches in the table below. If a sheet is folded once, the size of the two resultant leaves is called folio; fold it

* An explanation of the lithographic and gravure techniques will be found in the next chapter.

again and we have a quarto (4to); again, an octavo (8vo). Similarly, the terms 12mo, 16mo, 32mo, indicating that the page is one-twelfth, one-sixteenth, and one thirty-second respectively of the area of the original sheet, tell the number of times it has been folded. The terms themselves represent not actual sizes but the proportion of the page to the full sheet. They are, however, loosely used to indicate the shape of a book; thus a folio is a large tall volume, a quarto less deep but squarer, while an octavo returns to the proportion of a folio but in a smaller size. If the edges of a book have been trimmed, the width may be shorter by an eighth of an inch, the depth by a quarter of an inch, and these curtailments will be greater if the book has been rebound, since a fresh trimming is then necessary.

		Folio	Quarto	Octavo
Foolscap	17 × 13½	13½ × 8½	8½ × 6¾	6¾ × 4¼
Crown	20 × 15	15 × 10	10 × 7½	7½ × 5
Demy	22½ × 17½	17½ × 11¼	11¼ × 8¾	8¾ × 5⅝
Royal	25 × 20	20 × 12½	12½ × 10	10 × 6¼

Where the page varies considerably from all of the standard sizes, it may be referred to as 'small demy octavo', 'large foolscap octavo', and so on. In some cases no such designation can be found to apply and the actual measurements of the page must be given in inches or centimetres. For exact purposes this method is essential.

As a result of the introduction of machinery in papermaking it is possible to manufacture far larger sheets than the makers of hand-made papers could hold, and printers and binders, finding it cheaper to deal in the bigger units, have installed bigger machines to handle them. It may be safely assumed that, unless a hand-made paper has been used, the sizes of the sheets on which a book is printed nowadays are not crown, demy or royal, but twice or four times those sizes. The binder may cut them in half or quarter before folding them, or he may retain the larger sheet and fold it once or twice more. Thus what appears to be a demy 8vo (and is still known as such) may in fact be a double demy 16mo. This procedure is only adopted when extreme economy is required, for sheets folded so many times are liable to gape, and unless the paper is very thin, set a perilous strain on the bound book.

As a guide to the binder in arranging the sheets in correct sequence a letter or number (usually with some initials to identify the book) is printed at the foot of the first page of every sheet. These signatures, for so they are called, afford an easy means of ascertaining how many pages each folded sheet contains. In this book, for instance, the signature 1 appears on page 1 and the signature 2 on page 17, showing that each sheet contains sixteen pages. But it must be remembered that this does not mean that a sheet containing sixteen pages was the printer's unit. In modern books it is more likely to have been a sheet of thirty-two or sixty-four pages, cut in half or quarter before folding. In the books of past centuries, the printer with a far smaller machine might print two sheets of four or eight pages each and slip one inside the other to make his binding unit. Such a practice may often be detected by a study of the water-marks in the paper.

Since the terms 'page' and 'leaf' are occasionally confused, it may be observed that a page is one side of a leaf, and a leaf may therefore have two pages printed on it, one on each side. The first page of a leaf, the right-hand page of an open book, is called the recto of a leaf, and the second page, the left-hand page of the open book, the verso. When every page is numbered, the book is said to be paged; but when a number is given to each leaf only, the book is said to be folioed.

The size of type follows closely on the choice of format; the larger the page, as a general rule, the larger the type should be. Legibility is the first demand on a typographer, and if long lines are printed in small type the eye not only finds it difficult to pick up the beginning of each but also tends to lose itself in the middle. If economy of space is necessary, recourse may be had to double column, when a smaller type can, of course, be used.

The choice of type-face is more complex, though this problem is considerably easier of solution now than fifty years ago. The introduction of composing machines, by which fresh type is cast for each book from stock matrices, enables the printer to carry a far larger variety of faces than he could economically manage in the past, each of which has its peculiar characteristics. The common principle of composing machines is the control of letter matrices by an operator, who taps out his work, letter by letter, on a keyboard, thereby bringing the required matrix automatically into position. Molten lead is forced into it through a mould, and so the type is cast. This semi-mechanical process is considerably quicker than the picking up and placing of single letters by hand, and has another advantage in that fresh type is cast for each book, whereas by the older method the type not only had to be sorted and returned to its case after the book was printed but became worn and battered with frequent use.

The types used for books to-day may be recent designs or copies of the type-faces of the past, and it will be necessary to consider which of those available best suits the practical and aesthetic requirements of the work in hand. The appendix on pages 121–128 shows a selection of type designs from the earliest times, nearly all of which (and at least a hundred more) are now available for composing machines. A round clear type is appropriate for a school text book; an eighteenth-century type may well be chosen for an eighteenth-century biography; a narrow type will enable a large manuscript to be compressed into a book of reasonable size. Such are the various considerations which guide the designer in his selection.

Each different type family exists in a number of sizes. The old and picturesque names for these—nonpareil, brevier, bourgeois, pica and so on—have now given way to a classification by points, a point being one seventy-second of an inch. This measurement does not apply to the individual letter as it appears on the printed page, but to the whole of the depth of the body, that is from the top of a 'b' to the bottom of a 'q'. The text of this book is set in 10, the foot-notes in 8 point.

The book-designer, then, having chosen a type-face, proceeds to the appointment of different sizes of it for text, notes, chapter and page headings, index and so on. At the same time he settles the proportion of type to page, or in other words he decides on the length of the line and the width of the margins. Good printing has been well said to be nine-tenths a matter of good spacing; and nowhere is this consideration more important than in the proportion of the mass of the type to the paper upon which it is printed, i.e. to the margins of the page. The rules are much the same as apply to the mounting of a picture: there must be more space at the foot than at the head, or the type (or picture) will appear to be slipping down. In the same way, since the two facing pages form one picture to the eye, the inner margins together should not exceed each outer one in width, or the type will seem to be falling out of the pages in a lateral direction. A good proportion, therefore, of the margins of a page is: inner 1, upper 1½, outer 2, lower 3.

Often the page of type is leaded, that is, strips of lead are inserted between the type lines. This is sometimes done to drive out the book to a greater number of pages, but the effect may be ugly and disconcerting if it is not intelligently carried out. As a general rule, modern types are improved by leading, both in looks and legibility, whereas old face types are better when set solid. Leading may also be introduced to facilitate the reading of long lines, and it is frequently desirable in the setting of poetry with short lines, in order to balance the extra white of the surrounding margins.

The preliminary pages of a book—the title, contents, dedication, and so on—afford the designer more freedom than the primary dictates of legibility and directness allow in the text pages. The chapter headings also demand some special care. Modern taste for simplicity (often disguising mere poverty of imagination) has ousted the printer's ornament so common in these positions in older books. Nowadays it is usually a matter of good type-faces, rightly placed, but though one may miss the greater extravagance in detail of past centuries, it cannot be denied that most books to-day are competently produced.

The consideration of illustrations and binding must be left to succeeding chapters, but before we leave the subject of type it is worth remarking that all the typographer's efforts to construct an elegant book may be ruined by corrections made by the author on his proofs. To change the title at this stage, to cut out sentences or add them, may well upset the detail of the design and spoil the whole work from the artistic point of view. Corrections, too, are expensive to carry out, especially those which cause overrunning of lines and rearrangement of pages. The insertion of a single word may cause a compositor ten minutes work or more, moving words from one line to the next as far as the end of a paragraph and respacing each line in turn. Authors should satisfy themselves that they have finished writing their books when they are sent to the printer. Nothing is a better surety of this, or a greater boon to the printer in every way, than clean and tidy typescripts. Publishers who watch their pockets would be well advised to insist on them.

An author usually sees two proofs of his book. If corrections are likely to be extensive, or illustrations have still to be prepared to fit into the text, the first proofs will be in 'slip' or 'galley', that is, in long strips before the type is made up into page form. It is better economy, however, to proceed straight into pages, arranged in long slips or in folded sheets according to the methods of the particular printing house. On these the author makes what corrections he must, and adds page headings if they change from page to page. Headings which merely repeat the name of the book are useless; but the chapter and section titles may be employed, and if this instruction is given beforehand the printer can incorporate them in the first page proof.

The proof is returned to the printer, who carries out the corrections, and in due course a second proof or 'revise' reaches the author. Here he will be able to check the alterations he has made, and he will also find that a trained reader has raised queries about such matters as the clarity of his sentences, consistency of spelling and capitalization, and even accuracy of fact. This 'press reading' is a great boon to authors, all of whom fall unconsciously into error at times. It is a service traditionally carried out by the printer, although strictly it is outside his province, belonging properly to the publisher and the author himself (or somebody employed directly by him), since it is they who are responsible for the matter of the book, the printer's charge being the manner of its presentation.

A word may here be said about style. Grammar, punctuation, and to a large extent spelling, are not subject to fixed rules, and many authors have marked idiosyncrasies in these matters, while others have no standards at all. The rule of most printing houses is to follow the author where he shows a preference, but where he shows none, to impose the 'house style' and so at least achieve consistency. Certain points, such as the treatment of references, nearly all authors are only too glad to leave to the printer, and printing firms regularly employ copy-preparers who deal with these matters before the manuscript (as typescripts, as well as true manuscripts, are known) passes to the compositors. A neat and consistent typescript commands immediate respect, with a result that professional typists are even more instrumental than printers in standardizing punctuation, spelling, the use of capitals, and other such matters.

The compilation of the index normally falls to the author's lot and does not always receive the attention it deserves. 'The labour and patience, the judgment and penetration which are required to make a good index, is only known to those who have gone through this most painful, but least praised part of a publication', was the considered opinion of the eighteenth-century bibliographer William Oldys; and yet earlier Nicolas Antonio, the Spanish bibliographer, related as the dictum of a celebrated compatriot, 'that the index of a book should be written by the author, even if the book itself were written by someone else'. With the exception of cyclopaedias and dictionaries, almost every book that aims at being useful requires an index to make its store of knowledge accessible.

The material on which books are printed is nearly always paper, but occasionally vellum is used. The 'rag books' of the nursery are another variant. In the early days of printing, when manuscripts were commonly written upon vellum, it was natural that that material should frequently be employed for some copies of a printed book. But even then it was exceptional, since paper was in comparison much cheaper, and the large supplies of vellum necessary for whole impressions of a book would be difficult to obtain. In some instances certain parts of a book liable to hard usage, such as the leaves of a prayer-book containing the Mass, were printed on vellum.

The manufacture of paper is said to have been carried out in China in the early years of the Christian era, and was practised by the Arabs before the end of the eighth century. In the eleventh century the Moors introduced it into Spain, whence it spread through Europe, reaching England shortly before 1550. In former days paper was made almost exclusively from rags; but in modern times, and more especially since the abolition of the Paper Duty in 1861, the material which goes under the name of paper is manufactured from various vegetable fibres, including wood, esparto grass, and less commonly bamboo and straw. Wood forms by far the greatest proportion of the material used, and in its best qualities is as good as any but the finest rag. Esparto grass is favoured for its lightness and opacity.

Hand-made paper is still used for occasional fine books, but it is expensive both to produce and (on account of its limitations of size) to use. The printing of a few copies of a book on hand-made and a cheaper edition on machine-made paper has become rare in England; and the 'large-paper' edition, where the same type is used but with wider margins, rarer still. In France both practices are freely used, some books being issued simultaneously on half a dozen varieties of paper, to suit every pocket and predilection.

All paper is either laid or wove. There is no difference in the manufacture or quality, but laid papers, when held up to the light, show semi-transparent lines running close together in one direction, with heavier lines about an inch apart in the other. This pattern is obtained by the impression of wires at an intermediate stage of manufacture, watermarks being obtained in the same way. Both these kinds of paper are made in an almost endless variety of quality, tint and thickness. If left rough, they are known as antique. A smoother surface is obtained by passing them finally between rollers, and they are then known as machine finished, or, in a still smoother variety, super-calendered. For the highly glazed surface of 'art-paper' a special process of coating with china clay is introduced; this category is needed for the reproduction of fine half-tone blocks. With the object of bringing books within small compass the use of very thin paper is frequently resorted to, and the necessary qualities of strength and opaqueness, together with a pleasant silk-like feel, are combined with extraordinary success in 'India' paper.

The terms 'edition' and 'impression' are sometimes indiscriminately used to describe the number of copies printed at one time; in the sense now generally approved, however, edition refers to the state of the book, impression to the number. Thus an edition may consist of any number of impressions, so long as the type is not reset or the matter substantially changed. As soon as considerable alterations are introduced, or the type reset, a new edition is said to exist. A re-issue means that copies of an impression already on sale have been put on the market in a new guise and probably at a new price. The description 'limited edition' implies that no further issue will be made in that form, a virtue being made of the fact to give a rarity value to each copy. The hand-printer of fine editions will often limit the number according to how long he feels able to concentrate on his work the care and attention necessary to ensure perfection.

The process of stereotyping, by which plates are made from the type for successive printings, has been described in the foregoing chapter. Another method of reproducing books after the type has been melted is by photo-lithography from the printed pages, a process to be described in the next.

CHAPTER VIII

ILLUSTRATIONS

Until recent times the chief methods of producing illustrations for printed books were woodcutting, metal engraving, etching and lithography. But during the last fifty years the province of every one of these arts has been invaded by photography; and the various processes by which illustrations in black-and-white and in colour are now produced are bewilderingly numerous. All these methods, whether handicraft or mechanical, may be divided into three groups distinguished by the nature of the surface of the block or plate from which the picture is printed. In the first of these the design is in relief, like type, and, in printing, it is impressed into the paper. To this group belong woodcuts, wood engravings, and some of the modern mechanical processes such as zinc etchings and half-tone blocks. In the second group the lines composing the picture are sunk below the surface of the plate, and, in printing, the paper is pressed into these lines, so that the picture is in low relief upon the surface of the paper. By this, the *intaglio* method, are produced copper-plate and steel engravings, and certain of the photographic processes such as photogravure. The third group comprises pictures printed from flat surfaces, and includes lithographs and, again with the aid of photography, collotypes.

Although the printing of pictures from wood-blocks preceded the invention of typography, the printer of books in movable type did not at first make use of the art of the engraver—or woodcutter, as the maker of early woodcuts should perhaps be called—to illustrate the printed book. In fact, in its beginnings, the printed book had more affinity with a manuscript than with either the woodcut picture or the block-book, and it was to the illuminator that the early printer naturally turned for the decoration and illustration of his productions.

It was not long, however, before the printer perceived that the woodcutter's art might with advantage be utilized for the adornment of his books; and that not only for decoration in the shape of initial letters, borders and other ornamental adjuncts, but also for pictures which would elucidate the text or add to the attractiveness of popular works. These woodcuts consisted of a flat block of wood upon which the design was drawn and the surface of the wood afterwards cut away so as to leave the lines of the drawing in relief. Occasionally soft metal was used in place of wood. The height of the block being adjusted to that of the type, the picture or ornament could be printed in one and the same operation as the page of text.

The first printer to make use of illustrations was Albrecht Pfister of Bamberg, who about 1461–2 issued several popular German books containing woodcuts. But the history of illustrated books does not properly commence until some ten years later when pictures begin to make their appearance in books printed at Augsburg, where there existed a guild of craftsmen who cut blocks for printing playing-cards and pictures of saints, for both of which there was at that time a large demand. Ulm, another important centre of woodcutting, followed the lead of Augsburg, and the practice soon spread: Nuremberg, Cologne, Strasbourg and Mainz being among the chief German towns which produced illustrated books in the fifteenth century.

Copyright was as little recognized in pictorial art as in the world of letters, and a successful illustrated book was quickly copied or imitated, generally in other towns than that of its origin. The *Aesop*, printed by Johann Zainer at Ulm and containing two hundred woodcuts, was followed by half a score of other German editions, most of which were frankly copies; and the popular *Narrenschiff* (*Ship of Fools*) of Sebastian Brant, first published at Basel by Johann Bergmann von Olpe in 1494, with over one hundred illustrations, was paid the compliment of being reprinted in three other towns in the same year. Sometimes the pirated cuts were mere slavish imitations of the originals, perhaps copied by pasting one of the original pictures on the wood-block, in which case the copy would appear in a reversed form in the new book and so betray its origin. But the object was easy reproduction of pictures rather than fraudulent imitation, and details were freely paraphrased. Copies by a poor craftsman would show a distinct inferiority to the originals; but in the hands of a capable artist the new version might be a great improvement both in the handling of the subject and in technical execution.

The illustrations in Breydenbach's *Peregrinationes in Montem Syon* (Mainz, 1486) show a marked advance upon previous efforts in the art of woodcutting. The book also possesses a modern touch in that the illustrator, Erhard Reuwich, joined the pilgrimage as special artist to the expedition; and since the page of animals 'veraciter depicta sicut vidimus in terra sancta' includes a salamander, a unicorn, and a baboon leading a camel, it is clear that the special correspondent of the fifteenth century would have little to learn from his modern descendants. Shortly after this two of the most notable illustrated German books made their appearance at Nuremberg from the office of Anton Koberger: the *Schatzbehaltei* of 1491, and Hartmann Schedel's *Liber Chronicarum* of 1493. Michael Wohlgemuth was the artist responsible for the cuts in both. The latter, usually called the *Nuremberg Chronicle*, and perhaps the best-known illustrated book of the fifteenth century, has elbowed its way to the front by wide circulation, sheer bulk and a blustering profusion of woodcuts, many of the portraits being repeated over and over again for different persons.* The *Schatzbehalter*, with its full-page pictures, each with a story to tell, is really the more attractive book. An edition of the *Apocalypse* with full-page woodcuts by Albrecht Dürer appeared in Nuremberg in 1498.

Italy was somewhat later in adopting illustrations. The *Meditationes* of Turrecremata, printed at Rome by Ulrich Han in 1467, is believed to be the first Italian book in which woodcuts occur; but much better work may be seen in the eighty-two cuts which illustrate the edition of the *De re militari* of Valturius printed at Verona in 1472. Erhard Ratdolt, who printed at Venice from 1476 to 1485, is celebrated for his beautiful borders and

* An enumeration of the cuts shows that the book contains 1809 pictures printed from 645 different blocks. See A. W. Pollard, *Fine Books* (1912), p. 117.

initial letters; and a few books with pictures appeared both at Venice and other towns during that period. The use of woodcuts did not, however, become common in Italian books until about 1490, in which year Lucantonio Giunta published at Venice the first illustrated edition of Malermi's Italian version of the Bible. Some of the cuts in this book—there are nearly four hundred of them—were adaptations from the German Bible printed at Cologne by Heinrich Quentell some ten years earlier.

The most remarkable Italian illustrated book of the fifteenth century was the *Hypnerotomachia Poliphili* of Francesco Colonna, which Aldus, who was not given to the use of pictures, printed for Leonardo Crassus in 1499. This fine folio in its rich array of graceful and well-executed woodcuts is a striking contrast to the little Savonarola tracts and *Rappresentazioni*, or miracle-plays, which form the most characteristic illustrated productions of the Florentine press. These popular booklets, with their charming little woodcuts generally surrounded by a border having a white design on a black ground, had a vogue which lasted from 1490 to the middle of the sixteenth century.

In Paris, a stronghold of the trade in manuscripts, the printing press ousted the scribe less easily; and it was here, more than in most other places, that the printed book kept touch with the art of the illuminator. This is specially observable in the *Horae*, or Books of Hours, of which innumerable editions were printed in France between 1486 and the middle of the sixteenth century. In these books nearly every page is surrounded by an elaborate border, generally made up of small pictures enclosed by intertwining foliage or other decorative framework. The subjects may be either Old Testament types, biblical scenes, histories of saints, the dance of death, or even rural scenes and daily occupations. The small pictures were frequently on separate blocks, and so lent themselves to an almost infinite variety of combinations. Besides the borders, a larger picture, occupying nearly the whole page, was placed at the beginning of the several sections of the work, each of which had its appropriate subject. Many copies were printed on vellum, and the borders and pictures were often gilded and coloured in the style of manuscripts by an illuminator, who, when occasion demanded or fancy prompted, would overlay the printed ornament or picture with some entirely different design.

Some of the best of these books of private prayers are among the editions printed at Paris by Philippe Pigouchet for Simon Vostre during the twenty years from about 1490. Other prominent printers and publishers of them were Jean du Pré, Thielman Kerver, Gilles Hardouyn and Antoine Vérard. The last of these was one of the greatest of the early French publishers, and his numerous books are freely illustrated with cuts both new and old. In the *Horae* (1525) of the artist-printer Geofroy Tory the tradition of manuscript decoration is no longer dominant and the ornamentation is in full Renaissance style.

Several books printed in the Low Countries in the fifteenth century were finely illustrated in wood, and Colard Mansion, with whom Caxton worked in Bruges, experimented with engravings in copper, though without much success. The early English press is not remarkable for its illustrations or its decorative qualities.

Illustration from *Hypnerotomachia Poliphili* (Venice, 1499)

Et cũ itinxisset
panẽ dedit iu=
de symõis sca .

Cõstituerũt ei
trigita argéte=
os et exide. zc

Deus in adiutoriũ meũ intende Dñe
ad adiuuandũ me festina Gloria patri
et filio Sicut erat .ac.ãn. Assumpta.

Page of a *Horae* (Paris, 1498)

Such pictures and ornaments as were used were mostly either imported from the continent or derived their inspiration from foreign originals. The first English books in which woodcuts occur are *The Mirrour of the World* and the third edition of the *Parvus et Magnus Cato*, both of which were printed by Caxton about 1481. Caxton used illustrations in several other books, notably the second edition of the *Canterbury Tales*, in which the designs were at least of English origin, the *Fables of Esope* (1484), turned into English by Caxton himself and illustrated by one hundred and six pictures, and the *Golden Legend*, the largest and most ambitious of all his books.

Wynkyn de Worde used woodcuts more freely than Caxton, but he seems to have valued them rather as adding to the saleability of the book than as illustrating the text. Among the more prominent of his illustrated books are the fine folio edition of the *De proprietatibus rerum* of Bartholomaeus Anglicus and the *Morte d'Arthur* of 1498. Several of his small quartos have woodcuts, and he also printed a *Sarum Primer* with borders to every page and a number of small cuts. Pynson, like Caxton and de Worde, also issued a pictorial edition of the *Canterbury Tales*, but his illustrated books are better represented by the 1494 edition of Lydgate's *Falle of Princes* and the *Kalendar of Shephardes* of 1506, though it may be noted that the cuts in both are of French origin. The woodcuts, upwards of one hundred, in Barclay's English version of the *Ship of Fools*, which Pynson printed in 1509, are copies of those in the original Basel edition of 1494; sixty years later they were resuscitated for the edition which John Cawood published in 1570.

In the sixteenth century the talents of the foremost artists found expression in the printed book, and the illustrations of that period still rank with the best ever produced. Dürer, the greatest of these artists, served an apprenticeship to Wohlgemuth in his native town of Nuremberg. Hans Burgkmair, his contemporary, was of the celebrated art centre at Augsburg, as was also Hans Holbein, whose chief work, however, was done at Basel; while Lucas Cranach made his home at Wittenberg. Jost Amman, best known by his clever delineations of trades and occupations in Schopper's *Panoplia* (Frankfort, 1568), belongs to the second half of the century; and at the end of it Theodore de Bry and his sons were bringing out at Frankfort their wonderful series of illustrated travel books. Some of these artists, and notably Holbein, also designed book decorations in the form of initial letters and the beautiful borders which are characteristic of sixteenth-century title-pages. In the latter part of his career Pynson frequently placed his title-pages within ornamental borders, of which he possessed some good designs, and this feature also appears in the books issued in 1521 by John Siberch, the first Cambridge printer, who was brought over by Erasmus from the continent. From this date bordered title-pages become increasingly common in English books, though illustrations were by no means freely used. Foxe's *Book of Martyrs* (1563) was one of the most popular illustrated books of the time, and John Day, who printed it, also brought out *A Booke of Christian Prayers*, commonly called Queen Elizabeth's Prayer Book. This book, which has a pictorial border to each page after the manner of the French *Horae*, is a curious revival and the only English representative of that style.

The sixteenth century saw the woodcut at its best; but by the middle of the century a rival craft was beginning to assert itself. The art of metal engraving had occasionally been used for the illustration of books as early as the fifteenth century, but its sporadic employment hardly threatened the early supremacy of the woodcut, which held its own, aided, no doubt, by the fact that it could be printed with the text. But copperplate engraving, which appealed to the artist-engraver as a more sympathetic vehicle for rendering half-tones and shadow, steadily won its way, so that by the end of the sixteenth century it had nearly displaced the woodcut, which then practically disappears for the next two hundred years.

The effect of the use of metal engraving for book illustration was more than a mere change in the method of producing the pictures. It involved changed relations between text and illustrations, and resulted in a loss of homogeneity in the printed book. Metal engravings belong, as has already been mentioned, to the intaglio group of processes, and, since they require a different kind of printing machine, cannot be printed at the same time as the letterpress. Consequently, it will be found that the illustrated book of the seventeenth and eighteenth centuries possesses certain new features.

Sometimes, and more particularly in the case of fine books, the engravings were printed in blank spaces left for that purpose in the page of text, or were printed on thin paper and pasted into their places on the page. But since it was less trouble to print the engravings apart from the letterpress, they were usually worked on separate sheets of paper which were afterwards inserted between the leaves of the book or gathered together at the end of the volume. In this form, familiarly known as 'plates', the illustrations are no longer an integral part of the printed book. This practice was further encouraged by the circumstance that the inferior paper which had come into general use was unsuitable for the printing of line engravings. The woodcut border to the title-page also disappears, and instead the book is 'adorn'd' with an engraved title-page in which the brief title of the work is more or less lost in an elaborate design, frequently consisting of architectural features or heavy draperies in combination with allegorical figures and other 'properties' deemed appropriate to the subject of the book. An engraved portrait of the author was an obviously suitable *vis-à-vis* to the engraved title-page.

An early success in English intaglio illustration was Thomas Geminus's pirated edition of Vesalius's *Anatomy*, published in 1545 and containing several engraved plates by Flemish artists, as well as a fine engraved title-page. Among other English books illustrated with metal engravings Sir John Harington's version of *Orlando Furioso* (1591), containing forty-six full-page pictures, is one of the best examples of that period. During the seventeenth century pictorial illustrations were used very sparingly in this country, and the popular engravers, among whom were Elstracke, Marshall, Faithorne and Hollar, were largely occupied upon title-pages and portraits. The same was true of the continent, Poussin's fine frontispieces to the books of the Paris

Imprimerie Royale (founded by Cardinal Richelieu in 1640) being outstanding successes. Exceptions were a number of atlases, notably those of the Netherlander Blaeu, and a few books with etched plates of a descriptive character, such as those of Jacques Callot. In the eighteenth century, engraved illustration reached in France a perfection of taste and a technical virtuosity which have perhaps never been surpassed in any age or country. The work of Oudry or Fragonard, the *Fermiers Généraux* La Fontaine or the Boucher Molière, epitomize the exquisite magnificence of a justly celebrated civilization.

England, at that time, produced nothing comparable: the plates of Gravelot and his kind being largely derivative, and the native genius of Hogarth hardly extending its influence, until the end of the century, beyond the domains of the print market. In another direction activity in antiquarian, architectural, and topographical research resulted in the production of many large volumes on these subjects illustrated with fine engraved plates. In the latter part of the century Thomas Stothard, a prolific book illustrator of inventive fancy, was busy with plates for *Robinson Crusoe*, *Clarissa Harlowe*, *Tristram Shandy* and many other English classics, while illustrated children's books found a vogue in many countries. William Blake, in his very individual style, produced some of the most ambitious and beautiful of all book illustrations. He developed a technique of engraving the whole book, text as well as pictures, on metal relief blocks, a reversion in principle to the block-book of the fifteenth century.

Woodcuts had continued to be used occasionally in chap-books and other forms of popular literature; but, as they were generally either battered and hard-worn veterans of an earlier age or debased copies of old cuts, they contributed nothing to the survival of the art, which remained under a cloud until its revival at the hands of Thomas Bewick, whose cuts for Gay's *Fables* (1779), the Poems of Goldsmith and *General History of Quadrupeds* (1790) mark a new era in book illustration. The fresh life which the genius of Bewick and his followers infused into their art was more in the nature of a new development than a mere revival. New methods and principles were introduced, and henceforth we speak of the craft as 'wood engraving' in place of the old term 'woodcutting'. The great technical skill and delicacy of effect which the wood engravers attained brought their art once more into favour and inspired a distinctively English school of illustration.

In the nineteenth century the use of illustrations in books of every kind greatly increased. Although wood engraving was the principal process employed, all the other methods of pictorial reproduction continued in use, their number being augmented early in the century by the introduction of lithography. This new process, in which the design is either drawn upon or transferred to the face of a specially prepared stone which forms the printing surface, was discovered by a German, Aloys Senefelder, at the very end of the eighteenth century—the most important development in printing since the invention of movable type. For over a hundred years, however, it found little place in book-printing, if we except oriental works, in which it served to reproduce the writing and ornamentation of scribes, and musical scores, where it proved cheaper than the relief or intaglio

Engraved title-page: Bacon's *Instauratio Magna* (London, 1620)

Illustration in line by Aubrey Beardsley

methods, if somewhat inferior to the latter in the beauty of its results.

The first quarter of the nineteenth century was the golden age of those coloured aquatint illustrations inseparably connected with the name of the publisher Rudolph Ackermann. Primarily a print merchant, Ackermann commissioned such artists as Pugin and Rowlandson for the production of descriptive illustrated books on Oxford, Cambridge, London and the like, which have enjoyed as great a reputation in our day as in their own. Nor were others slow to follow his example and in a few instances to rival his success.

With McLean, a fellow print dealer, Ackermann was also prominent in another, and a peculiarly English, department of illustration—the sporting book. The lively drawings of Herring, Sartorius and Wolstenholme were mainly confined to the magazines; but *Jorrocks' Jaunts* and *The Life of John Mytton* displayed in book form the extraordinary talent of Henry Alken for making riders look 'Meltonian' and every horse a thoroughbred as fast as the wind.

The art of caricature was ably sustained by the satirical activities of Dighton, Woodward, Gillray and Rowlandson—the last one of the greatest of all English artists. His *Tours of Dr Syntax* were immensely successful and begat numerous imitations in a genre where the text was subordinated to—in fact usually written merely to accompany—the plates. The medium of these caricaturists was the line engraving, with colouring added by hand; but the tradition was developed, on less exaggerated lines, by George Cruikshank, Seymour and H. K. Browne, illustrators of Dickens, and others working in black and white. John Leech, however, on whose shoulders the Surtees novels rode to fame, returned in the fifties to the earlier technique, which had indeed remained constant in the sporting book field.

Steel engraving was used with early and conspicuous success by that neglected artist John Martin, whose illustrations for *Paradise Lost* (1827) and the Bible almost rivalled the fabulous popularity of his prints. This medium was also characteristic of the many Annuals, Keepsakes, Books of Beauty and the like which flourished expensively in the second quarter of the century. Their quality was fine and their manner so much to the taste of the age that many other volumes equally deserved the comment made on the illustrated edition of Samuel Rogers's *Italy*, that it 'would have been dished without the plates'.

Soon after 1830 the field for wood engraving was enlarged by the use of illustrations in weekly journals, and additional importance was given to this movement by the founding of the *Illustrated London News* in 1842. Books had their full share of this expansion. The mid-Victorians showed equal relish for the stirring scenes of Sir John Gilbert and the rural beauties of Birket Foster as rendered in wood by the brothers Dalziel; while the drawings of John Tenniel are familiar, from his felicitous association with Lewis Carroll, to every child in England and many in other countries. The middle years of the century, however, are best known for the work of the not too homogeneous group of illustrators in wood commonly identified with 'the Sixties'. Distinguished among these extremely prolific designers were Rossetti, John Everett Millais, Frederick Walker and Arthur

Boyd Houghton, and although much of their work appeared in such periodicals as *Good Words*, *Once a Week* and *The Cornhill*, they also illustrated a great number of contemporary books and provided the *raison d'être* for an even greater number of reprints and selections, many of a poetical or sentimental character. The unfashionable style of much of this outburst of illustration must not, however, be allowed to obscure the very high standard of craftsmanship almost universally displayed, nor the commanding brilliance of a great many of the designs themselves. The *English Illustrated Magazine*, founded in 1883, was a brave effort to revive the cause of wood engraving, and a good deal of delicate and beautiful work is to be found in its earlier volumes, as also in America in the *Century*, *Scribner's* and *Harper's* magazines. But the day of the wood engraving for ordinary trade books was done.

No other country equalled the volume of England's output of illustrated books in this century, though Russia produced a body of highly interesting material and France had eminent artists at work; among them Delacroix (an early and successful exponent of lithography), Daumier, Gavarni, Doré, Manet and Toulouse-Lautrec. The United States produced little that was original during the first half of the century, but in the second half the illustrated magazines began to provide that effective stimulus which they continue to exert to-day. Then, in the seventies, came the practical development of line engraving by photo-mechanical methods, and in 1880 the half-tone plate was perfected simultaneously by Meisenbach in England, Petit in France, and Horgan and Ives in America. Book and magazine illustration deteriorated sadly. It was not merely that the results of these methods were inferior, but their facility led to shoddiness of the worst sort. Exceptions, of course, there were: among them the pretty coloured work of Randolph Caldecott, Kate Greenaway and Walter Crane. Nor must the popular Cranford Series be forgotten, with its legitimate off-shoots and numerous imitators. The gifts of Hugh Thomson and his school in black-and-white illustration were considerable, and they were skilfully adapted to the new processes.

Aubrey Beardsley, however, was the first to exploit to the full the artistic possibilities of mechanical line engraving, and the reproduction of his drawings in several works of Oscar Wilde, in *The Yellow Book* and elsewhere among John Lane's publications, show the masterly use he made of it. At the same time, Ricketts and Morris were, each in his own way, rebelling against the encroachments of industrialism and rescuing the wood engraving at least for use in the 'fine' book field.

When we come to the books of our own century, it is difficult to select those which are outstanding in the field of illustration. All the processes, old and new, are employed, and a notable and welcome trend is the effort to blend text and pictures harmoniously. Photo-lithography, by which type and illustrations can be laid down together (usually on metal plates which have replaced the stone surface), afford special facilities for this, and in some cases, particularly children's books, the text is actually reproduced from handwriting. Even the unlovely 'art paper' plate bids fair to be ousted by the progress made, especially in America, in the printing of half-tone blocks on antique paper.

Copper-plate engraving is not common in modern books, though in the hands of J. E. Laboureur it has given us some of the loveliest illustrated books of recent times, such as Rémy de Gourmont's novel *Le Songe d'une Femme*. Laboureur, a disciple of Toulouse-Lautrec, is hardly less successful with his lithographs and wood-blocks—witness such a little masterpiece as the *Chansons Madécasses*—and his breakaway from the heavy French woodcut style, frequently balanced by equally overweighted type, brought a breath of fresh air into the art of the book in that country. It is in England that the wood engraving is most successfully exploited to-day, and of the many artists at work in this medium Eric Gill and Robert Gibbings may be picked out for their skill in combining illustration with decoration of the text and in harmonizing the 'colour' of the two constituents, type and blocks.

Auto-lithography, by which the artist works directly on to the stone, has been used in England recently more for the jackets of books than their inside, while photo-lithography and photogravure are still mainly confined to commercial printing. The latter process has, however, been used with great success in the books of reproductions, many of them emanating from Vienna. Collotype, the most sensitive of all photographic methods, is used for the plates in many English and American books where the extra expense as compared with half-tone blocks can be afforded. Its best use, often in colour, was found in Germany until a few years ago, but it has since, for various reasons, lost its popularity there.

Before we leave the subject of illustration, a brief description of the various processes may be acceptable to the reader. We have already seen that there are three kinds of surface from which an image may be reproduced—relief, intaglio, and surface or planographic. Instances of the first are woodcuts and mechanical line and half-tone blocks; of the second, copper and steel plate engravings; of the third, lithography and collotype. Photography may be applied to them all. Even with woodcuts it is not uncommon for a photograph to be printed on to the wood for the engraver to follow with his tool.

The relief method of printing illustrations is precisely the same as is used for printing from type; the raised parts of the block receive a cover of ink which is transferred to the paper. Mechanical line blocks are made by printing a negative on to a zinc plate coated with a thin film of sensitized albumen, which is then covered with a layer of ink. Where light has passed through the negative, that is in the black parts of the picture, the albumen is fixed. Where light has been obstructed the albumen can be washed away with water, and the ink with it. The zinc plate is next dipped in a succession of nitric acid baths, where the parts unprotected by the ink are etched away. We are left with a reproduction of the original image standing in relief, reversed of course, so that it bears the same relation to the picture printed from it as a photographic negative does to its positive.

It is obvious that in printing from a relief block those portions of the face of the block which come in contact with the paper will produce corresponding solid marks on the paper, whether they be lines, dots, or larger portions of the surface. Since the marks thus made must be solid black, or one tone of colour if a coloured ink is used, tints and shades cannot be rendered by this method; though the effect is approximately attained in wood engraving by the use of lines graduated in thickness and distance from each other so as to produce the simulation of tint. The problem of reproducing pictures composed of tints and light-and-shade (and not of lines) was solved by the invention of the half-tone process. This is similar to that of making line etchings, but, in taking the photograph for transfer to the metal plate, a glass screen, closely ruled with fine lines at right angles to each other, is interposed between the negative and the picture. The result of this is that the image on the negative is broken up into small dots which vary in size and density according to the amount of light reflected through the ruled screen by the different parts of the picture. The face of the plate and the resultant reproduction thus consist of a mass of minute dots which are not separately visible to the eye but by their varying texture give the effect of the tones of the original. This construction may readily be seen by examining one of these illustrations with a magnifying lens. In the lighter parts of the picture it will be noticed that the dots are small and distinctly separated by the white ground between them. In the middle tones the black and white are more nearly even, while in the shadows the texture becomes white dots on a black ground. In some of the work used in newspaper illustration, where a coarser 'screen' is used, this effect may be detected without the aid of a lens.

From the earliest days of book illustration colour has been popular. Copies of books in which the illustrations have been coloured are of common occurrence in all periods, and generally this addition is contemporary work. Sometimes this was done by or for the owner, but in many cases books were issued by the publisher with the illustrations either plain or coloured. Initial letters printed in colour occur as early as Fust and Schoeffer's *Psalter* of 1457; and in the *Book of St Albans*, printed at St Albans in 1486, the heraldic shields are printed in colours. But until the eighteenth century little attempt was made to print illustrations in colours, and most of the colouring was done by hand.

During the eighteenth century, however, a number of processes were evolved for colour printing: notable among the experimenters being Le Blon and his pupils d'Agoty and Lasinio. Some copies of Blake's engraved books show a colour-printed base. And in the lavish illustrated books of the Ackermann type the groundwork and paler tints were printed, preparatory to the detail colour being added by hand. This aquatinting was developed by J. C. Lewis from the earlier technique of Le Prince. Later came Savage and Congreve, followed by the enormously prolific and successful George Baxter; while colour lithography came of age about 1840 with the work of Day and Haghe.

The three-colour process is based on the discoveries of Newton, worked out by Clerk Maxwell in the middle of the nineteenth century and quickly adapted to printing technique. Three blocks, representing the primary colours, are employed. The negatives for these are taken through filters of coloured glass or glass cells containing coloured liquid, in addition to the ruled screen. Each of these light filters allows only certain colours to pass through to the negative and stops the passage of all others. The colours of the original are thus automatically dissected and grouped in three categories representing approximately the yellows, the reds, and the blues, each of which is contained on a separate negative. Of the three process-blocks made from these negatives that representing the yellow tones is printed first in yellow ink, over this impression the red block is next printed, and finally the blue. The various colours and tints of the resultant picture are formed by the combination of these three colours printed over each other and varying in proportion according to the density of the printing surface of the respective blocks. The use of the right amount of colour and degree of pressure in printing are important factors in the success of the operation. It is also essential that the register should be absolutely accurate, that is to say the three impressions must follow each other in exactly the same place on the paper, or the result will be the blurred effect occasionally seen in cheap prints.

The very opposite of relief printing is the intaglio or gravure method, and for this reason it cannot be used with type on letter-press machines. The ink is taken, not from the raised parts of the plate, but from those that are sunk. After the ink has been applied the plate is wiped, so that there is no ink left on the surface. The hand method of preparing these plates, being slow and expensive, is now rare, and has given way to photographic means. The plates are prepared in much the same way as relief blocks, an acid-resist protecting the necessary parts, in this case those which are not to be reproduced. There is no screen, but a grain is necessary so that the etched parts will hold the ink, and this is discernible under a glass.

Of the surface methods, lithography (stone-drawing) was discovered, as we have seen, at the end of the eighteenth century, and after a temporary decline it has now become increasingly popular. In this process the image is laid down on a specially prepared stone of porous quality, in a medium (such as a fatty chalk) which has an affinity for varnish ink but will reject water. The surface of the stone is damped and then swept by inked rollers; the damp parts of the stone reject the ink, but where it has remained dry, that is, over the image, the ink takes and is transferred to paper laid upon it. The image can be laid down either direct or from a transfer; and the process has been adapted to metal plates on which a fatty acid is held by a fine grain, obtained by rocking the plate with powdered glass. Photo-lithography is often used for reprinting books of which no type or plates are available, and various methods have also been developed by which plates are prepared direct from letter matrices, so eliminating all use of metal type.

Collotype is carried out in much the same way as photo-lithography except that instead of stone or metal a gelatine surface is used. It is the most faithful reproduction method of all, and also the most expensive. As with lithography and gravure, a grain appears in the reproduction and can be detected under a magnifying glass; and as these three grains, and the half-tone screen, are all different, we have here a method of recognizing the process used for any work.

CHAPTER IX

BOOKBINDING

I. *Hand Binding*

When books changed their form from the roll to the codex (that is, were folded into leaves) some kind of binding became a necessity. This for two reasons: to keep the leaves in their right order, and to preserve the outer leaves from damage. By the time the printed book made its appearance binding had been practised for a thousand years or so. Since the construction of a printed book was similar to that of a manuscript, the binding naturally followed the same model, and in essentials the subsequent four centuries have witnessed little change in the handicraft of binding proper. The evolution of edition binding and the 'cased' book is a separate story and will be considered in the second part of this chapter.

The operations of bookbinding fall into two main divisions: forwarding and finishing. Each of these is considered a separate craft. The forwarder carries the work up to the point at which the book is covered with the selected material, be it leather, cloth or other fabric; the finisher adds the lettering and ornament. The methods employed in forwarding a book have hardly differed in principle since the first days of printing, and it is mainly in the materials used for covering and in the decoration that the successive styles and fashions in bindings consist.

The process of binding a book comprises a long series of operations, all requiring a nicety of handling and judgment to produce the perfect result. Of the principal stages the first consists in folding the sheets, or if, as is sometimes done, the binder receives them already folded, in seeing that this has been correctly done. Next the sheets are collated, and in this the binder is guided by the signatures, the small letter or number at the foot of the first page of each sheet. The book is next beaten, rolled, or pressed, to give it solidity; after which it is ready for sewing. This work is done in a kind of frame, called a sewing press, the sheets being laid with their backs to a series of four or five upright cords round which the thread is passed on its way out and in along the back of each sheet. When the sewing is finished these cords stand out as horizontal bands across the back of the book, forming panels as seen in most books bound in leather. A book sewn in this manner is said to be 'sewn flexible'. In an inferior style of binding, grooves are sawn into the back of the sheets and the cords lie in them, so that the thread merely passes behind the cords instead of going out at the back and right round them. In this case the cords do not form bands on the back, and the back may consequently be smooth, unless, as is frequently done, false bands are put on before the volume is covered. If it is desired to avoid having bands on the back the book can be sewn on tapes instead of cords; a much better method than sawing the back.

After sewing is completed and the back has been glued up, the binder proceeds to the rounding and backing of the volume. The first of these processes gives the back a convex form and thus provides space for the extra thickness which that part of the book has acquired owing to the presence of the sewing thread; while the object of backing is to make a groove into which the back edge of the boards may fit and form a hinge on which to open. Both these operations are done with a hammer, and call for considerable skill and care. A fashion for flat backs obtained to some extent in recent years, under the influence of Cobden Sanderson. In this style the rounding and backing are omitted, and what is called a French joint is used in attaching the boards. These books have a certain neatness and compactness of appearance when new, but if much used the back is liable to become concave, causing the fore-edge to protrude, and the volume takes on a painfully broken-backed aspect.

Boards, cut to the right size, are now attached to the book by drawing the slips (the free ends of the back cords) through holes in them, after which the cutting and decoration of the edges are taken in hand. The treatment of the edges allows considerable latitude of choice, and like the style of binding is governed largely by the kind of book and the use to which it will be put. In most cases it is desirable that the top should be cut smooth, as this helps to keep out dust; gilding the top gives it a more solid surface and therefore affords better protection. A full leather binding will usually have all three edges cut and gilded, but in half-binding it is customary to leave the fore-edge and tail ungilded. In the case of first editions and books where special importance is attached to the width of the margins, the fore-edge and tail at least (if not the top as well) will be left entirely untrimmed. The same rule applies to early printed books. Books intended for reference should have all edges cut smooth to facilitate use; the edges may be sprinkled or coloured to prevent soiling, but the luxury of marbling may well be reserved for the adornment of ledgers.

The edges having been finished and the head-bands set, the book must next be covered. The principal materials used are leather, vellum, buckram and cloth. Embroidery, silk and other fabrics are also occasionally employed, but both for fine bindings and for books that have to stand hard usage there is nothing to equal leather of good quality. Much of the leather used for binding during the last hundred years has failed to stand the test of time. The durability of the older material is frequently seen in books that have been rebacked, where the new back has already perished leaving the original sides still in possession. This inferiority, due to faulty methods of preparation and the use of injurious chemicals, was the subject of investigation by a Committee of the Society of Arts some forty years ago. Their report (1901) has borne good results, and most manufacturers of binders' leather now supply skins guaranteed free from acid. But the binder must shoulder his share of the blame for the unsatisfactory condition of so many leather bindings. Too often strength is sacrificed to the over-rated virtue of 'finish'; the leather being so pared down as to leave no more than a thin layer of the outer skin, and this especially at the hinges where the strain is greatest and strength is most needed. Even Bedford, the best English binder of the nineteenth century, was sometimes an offender in this respect, especially with tree calf.

Morocco, which has no rival for fine bindings, originally came from southern Spain and Morocco and was made of goat skins tanned with sumach. Three varieties of it are commonly used to-day: hard grain, straight grain and levant. The first is perhaps the most durable, the last certainly the handsomest. The small goat skins dyed in various shades of red, imported from and named after the Niger country, are excellent material and the irregularity of colouring gives a pleasing effect; but the surface is not suitable for decorative tooling. Russia, that beautiful leather so much in fashion a century ago, is seldom used to-day: it is not durable and after a time it gets dry and friable, the backs and joints breaking away in a fine powder. Old calf is often very good material, but the modern product, though its smoothness and colourings are attractive, is less reliable, since the virtue has sometimes been taken out of the leather in the manufacture. Pigskin is the strongest of all leathers used in bookbinding and will stand much hard wear. It is therefore specially suitable for heavy volumes and books in everyday use; but as any attempt at dyeing involves loss of some of its qualities it should be used only in its natural colour. In the seventeenth and eighteenth centuries plain brown sheepskin was in general use for ordinary books, and it is sometimes found to be still in remarkably good condition. Roan, basil, and other modern forms of sheepskin are hardly likely to come out of the test so well, and should not be used for books of permanent value. Vellum, more in favour in the sixteenth century than in recent times, is not a kindly material for binding. Books bound in vellum, especially thin volumes, object to open freely and will not remain quiet when in use. Moreover it is much affected by atmospheric conditions, especially dry heat, and generally requires ties or other inconvenient devices to keep the book properly closed and prevent it from warping on the shelf. Buckram, cloth and what is called 'art canvas' represent the cheaper class of coverings. They are the usual materials for publishers' bindings, but they are also invaluable to the bookman who desires to keep his shelves tidy. Provided the sewing and other structural work is sound, these materials are sufficiently durable and comely to serve the purpose of the lover of books who cannot afford the luxury of leather. Opinion is divided as to the relative qualities of buckram and cloth, but those who elect to bind in buckram would do well to remember that the red colours are usually very fleeting.

A book entirely covered in leather is called whole or full-bound. A half-bound book has leather back and corners, and the sides are covered with cloth or paper. When only the back is leather, the book is said to be quarter-bound. A particular form of this style in which the back is of brown leather and the sides covered with crimson paper is called Roxburghe binding from its being the pattern adopted by the Roxburghe Club for its publications. Quarter leather with cloth sides and vellum tips to protect the corners makes a neat and useful binding for octavo books.

With the covering of the book the forwarding process is complete, and the volume is passed on to the finisher for lettering and decoration, which is mostly worked in gold. For impressing the letters and ornaments on the leather the finisher employs wooden-handled brass tools on the end of which the letter or ornament is cut in relief. These tools are used heated to a certain temperature, the exact degree of which is a matter of experience. Armorial stamps and large ornaments which require heavy pressure are applied by means of a press; but lettering and decorative designs built up of separate small ornaments are worked in by hand. For ornamental bands a roll which repeats the design as it revolves is sometimes used; and straight lines are put in with a similar tool called a fillet. In proceeding to work, the design is usually first schemed out with the tools in black on paper. This copy having been fixed in position on the book, the binder goes over it with the tools, stamping the design upon the leather through the paper. The impression thus left on the book is then painted in with glaire, after which gold leaf is laid on with a pad of cotton-wool, and the tools are again impressed exactly in the same positions to fix the gold. This being done, the superfluous gold is rubbed off and the book is polished and varnished as a finishing touch. Other and less common methods of decorating leather bindings are blind tooling (in which the design is impressed into the leather without gilding), inlaying with leather of different colours, painting, and staining. Embossing, in which the design is raised on the surface, is also occasionally used, but this technique, so beautifully employed by the French binders of the Romantic period, is now mostly relegated to blotters and the like.

The bindings of printed books have little connection with those sumptuous covers of precious metal, enriched with ivories, enamels and gems, which in olden days were wrought by the goldsmith for the preservation of valuable manuscripts. Wooden boards and leather—either calf, deerskin or pigskin—formed the humbler but more serviceable binding in general use for early printed books. In large folios the leather usually covered the whole of the board, which was often further protected against wear and tear by brass bosses and corner-pieces. Smaller books were sometimes half-bound; in this case the leather covered only the back and about two inches of the sides, leaving the rest of the boards bare wood. Many of these early books were sewn on double bands of thick leather, the thread going round both in figure-of-eight fashion. The leather covering was decorated by stamping it with various devices and patterns. The tools for this work were usually cut in intaglio, so that the device showed in low relief on the binding; but on some German books the design was impressed into the leather.

The decoration of Italian bindings consisted chiefly of interlaced patterns, while in France and the Netherlands panel stamps were largely in use. English binders of the fifteenth century were in the habit of decorating their books with a number of small dies arranged in bands and circles. But the bindings that came from Caxton's workshop usually had a border of triangular stamps, and the centre was divided by diagonal lines into diamond-shaped compartments, with a flower, griffin or other small ornament in the centre of each. Small dies were superseded by the panel stamp and about 1530 by the roll, a wheel tool which produced a continuous pattern in the form of a ribbon. Panel stamps frequently formed the complete decoration of a small book, while the roll, sometimes in conjunction with a panel, served for larger volumes. A common English panel binding at the beginning of the sixteenth century would contain on one side the royal arms, France and England quarterly, with dragon and greyhound as supporters, and on the other a Tudor rose supported by angels, with the arms of London and other accessory symbols. This pair of panel stamps, with certain variations, was used by several different binders, and frequently bore their initials and mark. A few pictorial panels also occur, but these were much less common here than in France. The roll, at first a broad finely-cut design, soon deteriorated into a narrow meaningless ribbon, and the extinction of stamped work followed closely upon this debasement. All these decorations were stamped blind.

The introduction of gold tooling on leather began a new era in the decoration of bookbindings. This art, brought from the East, was established in Italy towards the close of the fifteenth century, and soon spread into other countries. The patronage and taste of two celebrated collectors has contributed largely to the fame of sixteenth-century gilt bindings. Grolier and Mahieu were both Frenchmen; and although the former began collecting books during his early residence in Italy, while the latter has only recently been disembarrassed by Mr Hobson of his long familiar Italianization as 'Maioli', their bindings were executed in France and almost certainly in Paris. Neither of these two connoisseurs restricted his patronage to a single bindery nor his fancy to a single style: both were addicted to the incorporation of names and mottoes in their designs—a feature as characteristic as the Apollo medallion of the so-called 'Canevari'* bindings which were coming from a Roman bindery at about the same time. Grolier's and Mahieu's books have stylistic and technical affiliations both with each other and with other Parisian work of the period. Which are the more beautiful, whether either surpass the standard of their anonymous contemporaries, may be discussed *ad infinitum*: that their combined average of quality is hardly equalled by the work of any subsequent master will be disputed by few.

Indeed, from the middle of the sixteenth century, thanks to the encouragement of a long succession of royal and distinguished collectors, the binders of France attained a degree of excellence in the design and execution of gold-tooled work unrivalled in any other country. For a time little is known of the binders themselves, and the various styles are connected with the possessors of the books—Francis I, Henry II, Catharine de' Medici, Diane de Poitiers and others—rather than those who designed and wrought them. But with Nicolas and Clovis Eve, who bound for Henry III (d. 1589) and his successors, there begins a line of distinguished craftsmen who impressed their personality upon successive styles. The name of Eve is associated with bindings covered with small compartments composed of palm leaves or laurel sprigs; and many books of this period, especially those bearing a coat of arms in the centre, are enriched with a *semis* of fleurs-de-lis or other small ornaments. The books of the great collector De Thou (d. 1617) are, however, for the most part in plain leather, with his

* Whether or no Mr Hobson's attribution of this group to Pier Luigi Farnese be accepted, it has long been clearly proved that they have no connection whatever with Canevari.

arms, a chevron between three gad-flies, in the centre, either alone or accompanied by those of his successive wives. The characteristic of the work of Le Gascon, the seventeenth-century binder, is the use of *pointillé* tooling, in which the lines are broken up into dots, producing a particularly brilliant and delicate effect, especially on the red morocco which he mostly used. This style, which was very widely imitated, continued in fashion until about 1660. Padeloup le jeune (d. 1758), the most famous of a family of noted binders, was celebrated for his elegant *dentelles* or lace borders; one of his patrons was Madame de Pompadour. Derome le jeune (d. about 1788) followed in the footsteps of Padeloup and likewise gained fame by the beauty of his *dentelle* borders: he is perhaps the most famous binder of the eighteenth century, but the crime of sawn backs and cropped margins has somewhat sullied his reputation as a true craftsman in English eyes. French bookbinding, in common with other arts, suffered eclipse in the upheaval of the Revolution; but in the nineteenth century the work of Thouvenin, Trautz, Chambolle-Duru, Marius Michel and others restored the tradition of finished workmanship, though not always accompanied by the inspiration of originality. The besetting sin of modern French binding is an excessive tightness in the back, which prevents the book staying open.

The first binder in England to practise gold tooling appears to have been Thomas Berthelet, printer and stationer to Henry VIII. In an extant bill for books bound for the King by Berthelet in the years 1541–3 are instances of this new style: 'a New Testament in latyne and a psalter englisshe & latyne bounde backe to backe in white leather gorgiously gilted on the leather', others were 'bounde after the Venecian fascion', or 'covered with purple velvit and written abowte with golde'. English binders derived from the continent not only the art of gold tooling, but also their inspiration; and most English gilt bindings of the sixteenth century were either executed by foreign workmen or copied from foreign models. The leather used in England was nearly always brown calf or sheep; morocco, though known in France, was rarely employed in this country before the seventeenth century. A favourite style of ornamentation consisted of heavily gilt centre and corner-pieces, with the rest of the side either left plain or powdered with a small ornament. Many of the books bound for Archbishop Parker, who established a binder in his own house, were gilt in this fashion. Queen Elizabeth, a great lover of fine books, had a special liking for embroidered bindings and for books bound in velvet with gold or silver mountings; some of the former are said to have been worked by the Queen herself. These embroidered bindings, worked in coloured silks and enriched with gold and silver thread, were a specially English production. James I also had a taste for velvet bindings, but his more characteristic style is leather with the royal arms in the centre of a diaper of fleurs-de-lis or other small ornaments. At this time good work was being done both at Oxford and at Cambridge; and in his singular community at Little Gidding Nicholas Ferrar 'entertained a Cambridge bookbinder's daughter that bound rarely to show them that piece of skill'.

Other fashions included the fan style, consisting of a circular fan-like ornament in the centre with similar

Grolier binding on a Basel book of 1537

English 'cottage' binding on a Cambridge book of 1711

sections in the corners; imitations of Le Gascon; and mosaic bindings of inlaid leather. The second half of the seventeenth century produced the distinctively English style known as 'cottage', in which the framework at top and bottom of the design bears some resemblance to a low gable. This style is usually associated with the name of Samuel Mearne, who, though appointed binder to Charles II, was not himself a binder. The Harleian style, so called because it was used for the great collection of Robert Harley, first Earl of Oxford (d. 1724), consists of an ornate centre-piece, generally diamond-shaped with a broad tooled border. Roger Payne, one of the best and most conscientious workmen of the second half of the eighteenth century, has acquired a wider fame than any other English binder, partly owing to the curiously detailed form in which he presented his bills. He worked chiefly in russia leather and straight-grained morocco, and bestowed his most elaborate decoration upon the backs of the books, leaving the sides comparatively plain. His traditions were carried on by Charles Hering; Charles Lewis, who bound many of the Althorp books; and Kalthoeber, who revived the art of painting pictures on the edges of books under the gold. In this method of decoration, of which Edwards of Halifax is the best known exponent, the painting on the edges of the book shows only when the leaves are fanned out, and is completely hidden under the gold when the book is shut. Francis Bedford, at one time a partner of Lewis, was the most prominent craftsman of the middle years of the century, and in more recent times conspicuously good work has been done in the designing and execution of gold-tooled bindings by both amateur and professional binders. In this movement a leading part has been taken by Cobden Sanderson, Douglas Cockerell and Miss S. T. Prideaux; while Birdsall of Northampton, Rivière and Zaehnsdorf of London and Bagguley of Newcastle-under-Lyme have worthily maintained the high standard of the regular trade.

II. *Trade and Edition Binding*

The distinction between 'fine' binding and 'trade' binding is a double one: economic and technical. Down to the beginning of the nineteenth century, and decreasingly later, a gentleman's library would admit only books bound in full or half-leather; whereas to-day it might almost be said that the more new leather in a library, the less reading. Some fastidious booklovers, however, have always had their books bound to their own liking by their own binders, and to a very limited extent they still do. The ordinary reader takes his books as they come from the bookseller and cares little about the covers so long as they stay on. The modern book-collector has made a fetish of 'original condition' and never binds or rebinds anything.

The eighteenth-century habit of printing on the half-title or title 'Price 5 shillings, or 6 shillings bound' reflects clearly the practice of the preceding centuries. The man who—like the Frenchman of to-day—intended binding any book he felt worth keeping, bought it unbound; or in later years lightly put up in wrappers or paper boards, with or without a paper label. The general reader, who could not afford, or cared nothing for, the pleasures of calf gilt or morocco extra, bought it in the ordinary 'trade' binding, of plain calf or sheep or (before 1700) limp vellum, which was the equivalent of our 'publisher's' binding of to-day.*

The fact that these two types of binding were made of the same basic material—the skin of some animal—and made in the same way—by hand—must not be allowed to obscure the vital difference between them. One was tailored to fit, the other ready made.

The trade binding of the fifteenth–eighteenth centuries was not a publisher's binding in the modern sense, since it was executed for the retailer, not the wholesaler. Books were handled wholesale in sheets or quires; and the expense of binding—a considerable item in the total cost—was passed on down the line, printer—promoter—sharer—wholesaler (or such of them as might be involved in the publishing) to the retail bookseller, who merely kept enough bound copies to cope with his week to week trading.

This piecemeal system was completely, though not quite immediately, changed by two epoch-making events which took place between 1820 and 1835. The first was the application of cloth to the covering of books: the second the invention of a method of making cloth cases in quantity and independently of the volumes they were to cover. Cloth itself, which now effectively differentiates English and American books from those of the continent, arrived almost by accident: an amateur

* In the sixteenth and seventeenth centuries and well on into the eighteenth, trade bindings were seldom lettered on the backs. During the earlier years, books habitually stood with their backs inwards on the shelf; the title being written on the cut fore-edges of the leaves or on a slip of paper which was then glued along the edge of the board.

form of it being substituted by William Pickering in the early twenties for the paper boards which by that time covered all but the slimmest books during their chrysalis period. Archibald Leighton's subsequent development of book-cloth proper was carried to revolutionary success by the casing technique which cut the costs and multiplied speed, and by the achievement of direct gilt blocking on to the fabric, which abolished the paper label and opened up endless possibilities of decoration. Publisher's cloth had arrived to stay.

The technical difference between a 'cased' book and a 'bound' book lies chiefly in the method of attaching the cover to the leaves. In the bound book the ends of the cords on which the sheets have been sewn are laced into the boards, which are thus fastened directly and strongly to the book before the covering material is put on. In the other, the case is made separately—boards and cloth cut, the one applied to the other, the decoration (if any) and lettering stamped on—all by machines. The book is then set in the case, its mull back and tapes glued to the inner edges of the boards, the endpapers affixed—again all by machines; and the finished results are stacked up by thousands an hour.

It is evident that a cased cloth book will not be so strong as one properly bound. It was still more evident in 1830, when cloth binding was less efficient and conservative opinion hostile. Yet by the end of that decade cloth had not only established itself as the regular clothing in which most books* made their way across the counter. It had also convinced the public that it was

* Novels, owing to their special distribution methods and market, lagged behind other types of book in this respect.

Publisher's binding of the classic period

an adequate substitute, not merely a temporary stopgap like boards, for leather; and in so doing it had shifted once for all, from the retailer or the customer himself back to the publisher, the responsibility for providing a book's permanent outer covering.

The subsequent history of publisher's binding, apart from the numerous mechanical improvements, is part of the history of taste, with the 'yellow back', the 'juvenile', the 'gift book', and the 'part issue' providing lively exceptions to all contemporary trends. The delicate and beautiful designs of the 1830's and 1840's gave way to the lavish ornament and wider fabric range of the two succeeding decades. The 1870's and 1880's were soberer in all departments except fiction. The 1890's saw the final blaze of the 'three-decker' and a return of rich ornament in other fields. Finally, with the new century came the extreme simplicity of blocking which has been the general rule ever since.

CHAPTER X

THE HANDLING AND MISHANDLING OF BOOKS

Of the risks of destruction to which books are exposed, that of fire is the most formidable, whether it be by violence, as in the case of the Strasbourg library in 1870 and the University library of Louvain in 1914, or by the no less destructive agency of accidental conflagration. Of the latter there are many instances, from the wholesale destruction of books in the Great Fire of London in 1666, and the irreparable damage to the Cottonian manuscripts in 1731, down to the partial destruction of the Turin library in 1904 and the burning of the New York State library at Albany in 1911. But books are difficult material to make a thorough end of by fire. Church and state authorities discovered this when they endeavoured to destroy heretical books by means of public bonfires, and as John Hill Burton says, 'in the end it was found easier and cheaper to burn the heretics themselves than their books'. However, the destruction which fire fails to accomplish may readily be completed by its twin enemy water, for it is by no means an unknown experience that greater damage has been done to books by the water with which the flames have been attacked than by the fire itself.

Water, in the more rarefied and insidious form of damp, has been probably an even more effective agent in the ruin of books. In an acute form damp will in time bring a volume to such a point of decay that it crumbles away in powder; in a lesser degree mildew may ruin the binding and irremediably stain the leaves; while even a slight amount of dampness will favour the ravages of bookworms. These pests, more evident in their tracks than in their persons, are not often found except among books which are subjected to a somewhat humid atmosphere and are seldom disturbed. They are the larvae of a small beetle belonging to the genus *Anobium*, and have the appearance of a whitish maggot about five-sixteenths of an inch in length, with a dark brown head. In their silent progress some bore holes in all directions through the volume, while others confine their industry to the wooden boards of the covers, which they gnaw to powder. They show a discriminating taste in paper, for their attentions are conferred mainly upon books of the fifteenth and sixteenth centuries; they seldom risk their digestions by attacks on the modern stuff which does duty for paper. When they are discovered to be in possession, their activity may be discouraged by opening the book freely so as to disturb them in their tunnels. The book should then be treated with benzene or formalin, and shut up in a box for a few days before being aired off and returned to the shelf.

When the bindings of books are affected by damp in the form of mould spots, they should be well rubbed with a soft duster—not forgetting to open the book and rub the insides and edges of the boards, as well as the outside—and thoroughly aired before they are put back. The shelves may also receive attention by the application of carbolic acid or some other germicide. Good ventilation is one of the best preventives of damp, and in order to allow free circulation of air it is advisable that an interval of about half an inch should be left between the inner edge of the shelf and the back of the bookcase. While the bookcase is in question it may be noted that, since contact with a sharp angle is liable to be destructive to the bottom of a book, the arris—that sharp and true edge which is the pride of a joiner's craft—should be ruthlessly rounded off the front of the shelves. The question of glazed versus open shelves will depend partly on the taste, but more on the locality, of the owner. In the country there is very little to be said for glass doors: if they slide, they jam, and if they swing out, they are a continual nuisance, if not an active peril. In towns, where dust is heavy and smuts persistent, it may be held that ventilation and convenience are too dearly bought at the expense of constant dirt or the damage inseparable from daily dusting. Furthermore, books should not be packed so tightly on the shelves that they cannot be taken from their place without risk of damage to the binding; nor should they be allowed to stand so loosely that they gape open and let dust fall between the leaves.

Other enemies to the well-being of books are the fumes of gas, most noticeable on the shelves near the top of the room, which in time will reduce leather bindings to dust; central heating, which also robs the air of its natural humidity; and strong sunlight, which not only dries up bindings but also plays havoc with their colour. Last, though not least, spring-cleaning, when books are banged together with a will, making joints to crack and boards to part company, while the intelligent dust heads straight for the open window (so it is firmly believed); while afterwards the booklover has the consolation of being assured that the books have been put back on the shelves 'exactly as they were'.

The leather binding of a book that is in frequent use retains its suppleness longer than one which stands idle on the shelf. This is due to ventilation, exercise and the slight dressing of grease which it receives in being handled. If the leather is allowed to get very dry it loses much of its strength, becomes brittle, is liable to crack, especially at the joints, and the surface crumbles away. To keep leather bindings in good condition they should be treated occasionally with some lubricant. A good preparation for this purpose is a mixture of two parts castor oil and one of paraffin wax or paraffin ointment. Saddle-soap, lanoline, vaseline and furniture polish have also been used for this purpose. The first three are fairly satisfactory, but as the acrid odour of the last suggests the presence of an undesirable element it had better be avoided.

In taking a book from the shelf it should not be plucked forth by hooking the forefinger into the head-band, for it is by the repetition of this action that the head-band gets broken and the upper part of the back is torn so that it hangs loose and, presently falling off, is lost. In earlier days when books stood with the fore-edge outwards they fared no better; clasps and silk ties offered tempting tags wherewith to draw the volumes from their places, and it thus came about that many books were bereft of these really rather tiresome appendages. A better way is to place the forefinger firmly on the top edges of the book about an inch from the back and tilt the volume forward so that it can be grasped between the thumb and fingers. Or, the volumes standing on each side of the book may be tilted in with the thumb and finger just sufficiently to allow the book to be seized and drawn out without touching the top.

Though the extended use of machinery has long made the trimming knife, or plough, a commonplace of binding machinery, some publishers still persist in the affectation of unopened edges. For those readers condemned (usually at extra, rather than less, cost in the purchase of the book) to rectify this omission, an ivory paper-knife is recommended; and it seems necessary to state that neither a finger nor a hairpin is a suitable substitute. In the act of cutting the knife should be drawn down rather than pushed forward, or the edges may cut up roughly; and if the edge of the knife is drawn across the hair two or three times the slight lubrication thus applied will cause it to do its work more smoothly. In cutting the top edges special care should be taken to cut quite up to the back; a quarter or half inch left uncut and then torn when the book is opened is but too commonly seen.

Another point which deserves more attention than it usually receives is the method of opening a new book. If a book is to open comfortably and the leaves turn over freely, the back, which is rounded while the book is closed, must assume a concave shape when the book is in use. But the back of a new book is stiffened with glue, and if it be opened violently in any one place, with the leaves gripped fast between finger and thumb, the back will probably crack at that point, making an awkward angle; and, since the back cannot afterwards take the supple curve which is its natural form, the book will always tend to open at that particular place. To prevent this, a new book should be carefully opened throughout, before reading. The best way is to work from both ends alternately towards the centre, opening gently but firmly in the middle of each gathering. This can readily be found, either by counting to half way between each signature mark (at the foot of the first page of each gathering) or more simply by merely looking for the sewing. In the average octavo, for instance, one reaches automatically for page 8, page 24, page 40 and so on.

The dust jacket, which quickly becomes soiled and tattered, should be discarded immediately. It is intended for the protection of the book until it reaches the reader's hands, and for display purposes in the bookseller's shop; and its preservation is a matter of concern only to the omnivorous librarian on the one hand and the more fanatical collectors of modern first editions on the other.

A book, having been carefully cut, properly opened and denuded of its temporary trimmings, is entitled to yet further consideration. In reading, it should not be held near the fire or the boards will warp; nor should it be left lying in the sun, for the same reason. Then there are various ways of keeping the place when reading the book. It can be laid face downwards—the commonest misdemeanour—or it can be dog's-eared, by turning down the corner of the leaf; or, following the habit of a certain schoolboy when absorbed in Henty, the corner of the leaf may be pinched off as it is turned over. Some people have even been known to tear out each page when read, and throw it out of the window. A slip of paper, however, is a simple and inexpensive alternative to any of these barbarous practices.

APPENDIX

THE DEVELOPMENT OF TYPE FACES

The following paragraphs are composed in the types they describe. Up to and including the eighteenth century, modern versions are shown, not always exact copies but based in spirit upon their prototypes. The paragraph illustrating the transitional letter of Sweynheym and Pannartz is set in the "Subiaco" type based on their design which Mr St John Hornby had cut for the Ashendene Press in 1901. The Garamond old face is set in Linotype "Granjon". All the nineteenth-century types shown are set in original material (including Morris's own type) in the possession of the Cambridge University Press, and the remaining paragraphs are composed from Monotype matrices.

Until the nineteenth century, only contemporary types were used; the first reversion to the designs of earlier times came with the revival of "old face" in the 1840's, and to-day printers employ the designs of the present and the past more or less indiscriminately. Naturally, not all the types cut by the typefounders of the past have been retained in use or revived. Each age has its characteristic style, of which the best examples alone are thought worthy of imitation.

The type face is only part of the whole of typographic design. Arrangement, spacing, paper, ink, are hardly less important, and all must be considered together in assessing the work of a printer or an age.

Gothic

The types used by the earliest printers were imitations of the Gothic handwriting which in various forms obtained all over Europe at the time. Types of Gothic character are now little used except in Germany. In England after the seventeenth century they continued to find service for bold headlines, a practice surviving in the titles of certain newspapers.

Conrad Sweynheym and Arnold Pannartz introduced printing into Italy, setting up a press at Subiaco in 1465. Their type, though considered fundamentally Gothic, shows the influence of the humanistic handwriting that was favoured by Renaissance scholars in Italy, & it thus paved the way for the pure romans that followed.

EARLY ROMAN

For his editions of Eusebius in 1470 Nicolas Jenson used the first pure roman type, of which the lower-case letters are clearly based on pen drawings. The capitals follow the inscriptional letters of the Romans. The type here shown, Bruce Rogers's Centaur, is broadly based on the Jenson letter, a characteristic of which is the e with the diagonal bar.

Aldus Manutius used for the printing of Cardinal Bembo's tract "De Aetna" (1495) a type which he later improved and which has been recently recut under the name of Bembo. Aldus's calligraphic romans were taken as a model for most sixteenth- and seventeenth-century types—French, Dutch, English and Italian.

ITALIC

Aldus was responsible for the first italic type, designed for use in a pocket edition of Latin authors. This is a later and more successful italic designed by Ludovico Arrighi in 1522, imitating (as Aldus did) the chancery hand. It will be noticed that upright capitals were used at first.

Another italic in the chancery style was cut for Antonio Blado, a printer of Rome. It was not until the middle of the sixteenth century that italic was used in association with roman; now, though a few books are set wholly in italic, its normal use is for emphasis, book titles and foreign words, occasionally for display.

OLD FACE

The roman cut by the Paris typefounder Claude Garamond (died 1561) was based on Aldus's types and was consequently not free of calligraphic touches. They were a penman's letters, not an engraver's, and became the prototype of the "old face" which reached England from Holland in the mid-eighteenth century.

The finest of the Dutch typefounders of the seventeenth and eighteenth centuries was Christopher van Dyck of Amsterdam. The Elzevirs used his types exclusively and a stock of them was imported by the Cambridge Press where they were used in *some of the most beautiful English books of the early eighteenth century.*

The first great English typefounder was William Caslon, who issued his earliest specimen sheet in 1734. His types were based on Dutch models but had definite characteristics of their own; they are less regular individually, but give an agreeable appearance in mass. *Though they suffered a temporary eclipse after his death, they have been popular in England ever since.*

John Baskerville of Birmingham, the second eminent English typefounder, was contemporary with William Caslon. His fine, precise types brought old face to its aesthetic climax, and England to the forefront of the typographical world. *The influence of his letter can be traced in all modern faces that followed.*

MODERN

Modern types had their roots in France at the end of the seventeenth century, one of the earliest examples being this design of Pierre-Simon Fournier, cut in 1745. Characteristics of the modern face are fine and longer serifs, a greater accent on thick and thin strokes, *and a pronounced vertical stress.*

The type of John Bell, in which this book is set, retains some old face characteristics, but it is predominantly modern and may be acclaimed as the first English modern face. It was cut by Richard Austin in 1788 *for the famous publisher, printer and bookseller after whom it is now named.*

The types designed by Giambattista Bodoni of Parma show the influence of many predecessors, including Fournier and Baskerville; but they are nevertheless markedly original. They take the modern face, with its tall body, its contrast of thick and thin, its mechanical curves and fine serifs, *as far as it can well go.*

NINETEENTH CENTURY

The main feature of nineteenth-century type design was the development in many forms of the "old style" face. These were based upon Caslon's design, but pared of its irregularities and so of all its character. In its best forms, as in this paragraph, old style is at least easy to read: *in its worst (such as Cheltenham) it is insufferable.*

Besides his particular old style face every printer in the nineteenth century carried a "modern", a modified and less dazzling form of the Bodoni letter. These and possibly a version of Caslon old face, with a galaxy of ornamental initials and display founts, *made up his typographical equipment.*

William Morris's Golden type (1890) went back to Jenson's letter, but was neither a creditable advance nor a good copy. It set a fashion in archaistic types of poor scholarship and little beauty, sported by the more pretentious printers for the next twenty years.

TWENTIETH CENTURY

A welcome revival of sane type design came with the cutting of Monotype Imprint in 1912. Like the old style faces it was based on Caslon's letter, but it is bolder, and, having been designed primarily for use in a periodical, carries short descenders. *It is a workmanlike type, not mannered, very readable.*

One of the most prolific of modern type-designers is Frederic Goudy, an American. This letter of his, Goudy Modern, was designed in 1921; in contrast with Imprint it carries long ascenders and descenders, and though it has eighteenth-century associations *it is nevertheless a fresh and lively type.*

Most original of twentieth-century designers is Eric Gill, whose successful book type, Perpetua, reveals an artist's fresh solution of the old problem of letter-form. As one would expect, it is primarily an engraver's answer, and the inscriptional capitals have great beauty. *The italics are less sloped than usual.*

BOOKS FOR FURTHER READING

PRINTING

BLADES, WILLIAM. The Biography and Typography of William Caxton (1877).

The British Museum Catalogue of Books printed in the Fifteenth Century (Introductions).

DE VINNE, THEODORE. The Practice of Typography: 4 vols. (New ed. 1914–21.)

DUFF, E. GORDON. Early Printed Books (1893).

—— The Printers, Stationers and Bookbinders of Westminster and London, 1476–1535 (1906).

—— The English Provincial Printers, Stationers and Bookbinders to 1557 (1912).

GREENWOOD, DAVID and GENTRY, HELEN. Chronology of Books and Printing (2nd ed. 1936).

HANSARD, T. C. Typographia (1825).

JOHNSON, A. F. Type Designs: their History and Development (1934).

LEGROS, L. A. and GRANT, J. C. Typographical Printing Surfaces (1916).

MORISON, STANLEY. Four Centuries of Fine Printing (1924).

—— Modern Fine Printing (1925).

—— Type Designs of the Past and Present (1926).

—— German Incunabula in the British Museum (1928).

—— John Bell: a Memoir (1930).

NEWDIGATE, B. H. The Art of the Book (1938).

The Nonesuch Century (1936).

POLLARD, A. W. Fine Books (1912).

REED, T. B. Old English Letter Foundries (1887).

SCHOLDERER, VICTOR. Greek Printing Types, 1465–1927 (1927).

A

STRAUS, RALPH and DENT, R. K. John Baskerville (1907).

TIMPERLEY, C. H. A Dictionary of Printers and Printing (2nd ed. 1842).

UPDIKE, D. B. Printing Types: their History, Forms and Use. 2 vols. (2nd ed. 1937).

WROTH, LAWRENCE C. The Colonial Printer (2nd ed. 1938).

PUBLISHING & BOOKSELLING

KNIGHT, CHARLES. Shadows of the Old Booksellers (new ed. 1927).

LEHMANN-HAUPT, H. (editor). The Book in America (1937).

MUMBY, F. A. Publishing and Bookselling (1930).

UNWIN, STANLEY. The Truth about Publishing (1926).

ILLUSTRATION

CURWEN, HAROLD. Processes of Graphic Reproduction in Printing (1934).

GAMBLE, C. W. Modern Illustration Processes (1933).

HARDIE, MARTIN. English Coloured Books (1906).

HIND, A. M. Short History of Engraving and Etching (3rd ed. 1923).

—— An Introduction to the History of Woodcut. 2 vols. (1935).

REID, FORREST. The Illustrators of the Sixties (1928).

BOOKBINDING

CARTER, JOHN. Publishers' Cloth: an Outline History, 1820–1900 (1935).

COCKERELL, DOUGLAS. Bookbinding and the Care of Books (1901).

FLETCHER, W. Y. English Bookbindings in the British Museum (1895).

GOLDSCHMIDT, E. P. Gothic and Renaissance Bookbindings (1928).

LEIGHTON, DOUGLAS. Edition Binding (1935).

PRIDEAUX, S. T. An Historical Sketch of Bookbinding (1893).

SADLEIR, MICHAEL. The Evolution of Publishers' Binding Styles (1930).

BIBLIOGRAPHY

ESDAILE, ARUNDELL. Student's Manual of Bibliography (1931).

McKERROW, R. B. Introduction to Bibliography (1927).

PAPER

HUNTER, DARD. Paper-making through Eighteen Centuries (1930).

PERIODICALS

Bibliographica: Papers on Books, their History and Art (1895–97).

The Dolphin: a Journal of the Making of Books (1933–).

The Fleuron: a Journal of Typography (1923–30).

The Library: *now* the Transactions of the Bibliographical Society (1889–).

Typography (1936–).

Signature: a Quadrimestrial of Typography and Graphic Arts (1935–).

INDEX

Places have been indexed under countries. Printers and publishers, bookbinders, illustrators, are to be found under those headings; type founders and designers will be found under 'type design'.

Device used by the Cambridge University Press in the eighteenth century